BROKEN
SOULS

BROKEN SOULS

A Christian Approach
to Spiritual Healing

DR. MIKE DUFFY

ISBN - 979-8-9988466-0-1 (paperback)
ISBN - 979-8-9988466-1-8 (ebook)

Unless otherwise stated, all Scripture quotations come from the King James Version. Public Domain.

Editing by Edward Thal
Cover design and typesetting by Jenneth Leed, JennethLeed.com

TABLE OF CONTENTS

Acknowledgement...9

Introduction 11

1. From the Wounds of Personal Trauma to the
   Healing Power of a Loving God.............................. 17

2. Building a Life On a Solid Foundation 23

   Salvation is Our Solid Foundation for Spiritual Life 24

   Sanctification is Our Normal Christian Life Experience 28

   Submission is the Way to Go 31

3. Stories of Radical Transformation 35

   The Maniac of Gadara... 37

   A Terrible Life – Powerless Against Sin.............................. 40

   A Lunatic Son... 41

   The Transforming Power of Christ 42

4. The Vast Scope of Mental Illness:
   Its Wounds and Scars.. 47

   Physical and Moral Wounds 47

   Understanding Trauma.. 49

   Processing Trauma and Grief.. 51

5. The Recognition of Mental Illness 53

   The Destructive Stigma, "Who Is At Fault?" 54

   Mental Illness and the Christian Community..................... 56

   A Perspective on Mental Illness – Public and Private........... 62

6. Scriptural Admonitions to Discipline the Mind......... 63

   Competing Voices 63

How We Discipline Our Minds, Our Thinking Processes and Thought Patterns 65

Think on These Things 67

Paul's Four Step Program from Romans Chapter 6 72

Hide the Word in Your Heart 74

Behavior Is Driven by Thought! Our Thinking Leads to Action 77

7. Church Ministry 79

Making Disciples 79

Overcoming the Stigma of Mental Illness 81

Reviewing This Ministry 82

Develop a Pastoral Culture in the Church 85

Confirm the Pastoral Role 86

8. Spiritual Warfare 93

The "World" 94

The "Flesh" 95

The "Devil" 97

The Whole Armor of God 97

9. Therapeutic Exercises 103

Understanding the Grief Cycle 109

Accepting Comfort and Consolation 111

Commonly Recognized Treatments and Remedies 113

Non-medical Therapies 116

A Final Thought 119

About The Author 123

References 125

"Come unto me, all ye that labour
and are heavy laden, and I will give you rest."
Jesus Christ – Matthew 11:28

ACKNOWLEDGEMENT

It is with profound gratitude and appreciation that I acknowledge my good friend and published author Edward Thal for the major contribution he has made to this book. Our discussions about conditions in the congregations of churches, the vast content of the Bible regarding the issues we address, and his wisdom and insight from his personal experience have helped focus our thoughts and writings about this much needed topic.

INTRODUCTION

MY PERSONAL EXPERIENCE IS THE MOTIVATION FOR this book. It has been a slow process for me to recognize that I am not alone in suffering from an invisible ailment that burdened me before my salvation in Jesus Christ and somehow stayed with me after my salvation (though to a lesser degree). In this I am more fortunate than many others with similar ailments because my healing, though not yet complete, has been less fraught than some whose difficulties are either self-imposed or imposed by fellow Christians, invariably well-meaning but unaware of the nature of the problem and how to deal with it.

It will surprise many who know me as a Christian devoted to Jesus Christ, and those who are familiar with my very active ministry spanning several decades, that I have been handicapped for much of my life by an ailment categorized in medical literature as Post Traumatic Stress Disorder (PTSD).

PTSD is a mental health condition first identified and categorized in 1980 (after the Vietnam War) by the

American Psychiatric Association and usually associated with both soldiers and civilians who experienced the horrors of war. In the First and Second World Wars it was called "shell shock," a condition that resulted from living through extremely stressful or terrifying events. Symptoms may include flashbacks, nightmares, severe anxiety or uncontrollable thoughts about an event, or physical reactions to circumstances that trigger fears or emotions linked to a traumatic memory.

In my case the primary presenting condition is extreme claustrophobia—fear of being enclosed in a small space or being constricted in any manner. For many sufferers, symptoms of negative changes in thinking and emotions are more severe and may include ongoing fear, self-blame, guilt, anger, shame, detachment from family and friends and emotional numbness, being easily startled or frightened, always on guard for danger, irritability, aggressive and often self-destructive behavior. Physical reactions may occur, such as sweating, rapid breathing, fast heartbeat or trembling (so-called "panic attacks").

My own PTSD was born and nurtured in my mind and emotions as a small child who suffered the often irrational, destructive, traumatic and even terrifying circumstances of living in a home alongside my mother and siblings, with an alcoholic father. Some measure of relief came only after years of constant fear and upheaval when my father abandoned our family. After hitting bottom on Skid Row in Chicago, he entered and embraced an Alcoholics Anonymous

Twelve-Step program, where he was at last delivered from the death grip of alcohol addiction.

Against this background I entered the world as a young adult, a little "shell shocked" but optimistic; was married, then welcomed a first child, unaware that scars from my childhood lay somewhere deep inside me even as I went off to fight the war in Vietnam! To say that the horrors of that war experience worsened my inner condition would be an understatement. To this day, like so many fellow soldiers, I still lean on support from the Veterans Administration medical system.

Now retired, living and attending church in Georgetown, KY, a recent conversation with a good friend brought my disability very much to mind. My Christian brother was burdened by an awareness that some in our church (perhaps many in a congregation of several hundred) continue to hurt and suffer from the effects of past life events that they are fearful about exposing because others might view them in a negative light. Or their inner personal torments are often so severe that merely naming them can trigger familiar, unwelcome, and overwhelming emotions.

As we continued our discussion, we concluded that born-again believers bearing terrible inner scars from childhood traumas of physical or sexual abuse or abandonment may find themselves trapped in a singular area of neglect in an otherwise caring and loving Christian community.

Recognizing and adequately addressing the consequences of such neglect in the lives of these sufferers within the

Body of Christ, who are hindered in their relationships with God and with other believers, should surely be a normal component of our collective walk with God. But the question immediately arises: how should we minister to those whose ailments are invisible? More to the point, what should the Christian response be to those whose disabilities, once exposed, seem less like obvious handicaps (broken limbs, physical deformities, or serious illnesses like cancer), and more like sins—depression, despair, mood swings, and feelings of guilt or unworthiness?

My friend summarized this dilemma: "It's a major problem for Christians when a fellow Christian confesses to (for want of a better descriptive) soul weakness, or soul distress. It seems so alien within the Body of Christ! And so, the sufferers suffer in silence."

Probing deeper to focus our understanding and response to this condition produced a list of questions:

1. Is this suffering person saved or lost?
2. Are we dealing with sins or with symptoms of something else?
3. How should we define and respond to an inner (non-physical) wound that may not be the fault of the person we are seeking to help?
4. Are church leaders capable of providing help or should they defer to medical professionals?
5. How should fellow believers be informed of such a condition, if at all?

6. How will fellow believers respond to, or retreat from, awareness of such a condition?

7. Will appropriate treatment result in ultimate healing (elimination of the issue) or will the condition require ongoing management?

8. Will exposure of this problem leave a scar and what positive or negative consequences may result?

9. Is demonic oppression a possibility?

10. Is the church uninformed or not interested?

11. Does the Bible provide answers to these questions?

There are remedies available, but they must be appropriately applied. Consider the following:

1. In the process of sanctification, we are taught to refocus from self towards serving others. That is a wonderful transformation, guided by the Holy Spirit and the Word of God.

2. In a secular 12-step program one progresses through each step, moving from a life of selfishness and self-indulgence to a life of service. The AA's say, "You've got to give it away to keep it!"

3. In either case—sanctification or a 12-step program—the goal is a change of focus resulting from mental activity that will keep the individual from reverting (relapsing) back into a life of painful defeat.

4. Romans Chapter Six presents a template for inner transformation that could be utilized by Christian

counsellors in assisting traumatized individuals to overcome their disability. We could say it is the Christian 4-step program!

a. Know: verses 1-10
b. Reckon: verses 11-12
c. Yield: verses 13-20
d. Grow (experience the fruitfulness of resurrection life): verses 21-23

We will expand on this interesting concept in Chapter 6, and address important technical issues in Chapters 8 & 9. In the first chapter I share a testimony of my journey from personal trauma to healing through faith in Christ.

CHAPTER 1

From the Wounds of Personal Trauma to the Healing Power of a Loving God

MY STORY IS ABOUT A JOURNEY FROM SPIRITUAL death and darkness to spiritual life and light by God's grace through faith in Jesus Christ.

Everyone experiences hurt, but differences in our mental health are determined by how we respond to traumatic adversity. Sometimes we are comforted and process the pain in a healthy manner; at other times, the pain is not properly processed. That is, the normal emotional response cycle is interrupted or stalled.

In my case, response to traumatic events began to change and heal only after my conversion to Christ, being born-again into the family of God. But the process has been slow and incremental.

From a young age, long before Christ entered my life, I experienced the pain and suffering that accompanies the loss of loved ones, beginning with my grandpa, the first death I remember. Then the loss of my best friend from childhood, hit by a train the same weekend I got married. It left me in deep despair outside the funeral home. Other deaths were equally disturbing—a stepsister by suicide; the suicide of my cousin Eddie with whom I served in Vietnam; finding my mother dead in her home; having to pull the plug on my barely-alive father; and spending time with my younger brother the day he died. Each of these events was traumatic in their impact and each evoked a different emotional response.

Growing up in an alcoholic's home brought much heartache and trauma! The verbal and physical war between mom and dad, often in our presence, was terrifying. Dad's seeming disdain for my older brother was often manifested in verbal and physical abuse. The conduct of my parents became common knowledge in our community and this shame and stigma was almost as hard to bear as the tumult of our home environment. Life takes on dark tones for a child whose father is known as a drunkard. In an ironic twist, my parents shared ownership of a tavern where many of the residents of our community gathered and sometimes witnessed their mutual anger. When dad finally left our home in the back of an ambulance, and a divorce followed, mom did what she could to care for my two brothers and me, but we mostly grew up like orphans, left to fend for ourselves. There was trauma galore, and little comfort or direction!

Then came my deployment to Vietnam as a 20-year-old husband and father of a first child, a week after he was born, introducing a different kind of trauma. Leaving my wife of a year-and -a-half, and my baby son, indelibly etched the despairing moment in my mind. As I walked away from our home to an uncertain future in a combat zone I was overcome by feelings of helplessness and hopelessness. A deep sense of loss enveloped me. I was convinced that I would not be coming home again; ever! Friends and classmates had died in Vietnam, and now I was being deployed to fight with an infantry battalion of the 82nd Airborne Division. The war was at its peak.

My experience in that deployment added further layers of trauma. On the very first day, as I arrived with others at our base camp, I watched as the body bag containing a young lieutenant was emptied of blood and placed into the back of a vehicle to send him home. The red currency of freedom soaking into the sand made me understand the cost for the first time. Would it be me in that bag one day? My duty as a Jeep driver for the S-1 Officer brought with it a constant anxiety of the probability of imminent gun-fire or explosion. Then, as battalion casualty clerk, which required me to articulate in written form the circumstances surrounding the death of a soldier, to share with their loved ones back home, one trauma added to another trauma. Writing a "letter of condolence" brought with it the desperate sorrow and sense of grief that the family would soon experience!

Many of the casualties I followed as the medivac choppers hurried the wounded and dying to field hospitals were our "tunnel rats" who pursued the enemy in their underground bunkers. It was highly dangerous work. Unsurprisingly, my PTSD began to show up in the form of claustrophobia that despite numerous therapeutic interventions continues to impact me to this today.

There was a different inner response to the major health problems I suffered, and those experienced by loved ones. It was a sudden shock when our granddaughter was diagnosed with retinal blastoma (eye cancer). So young, at just seventeen months! Then the daughter of one of my best friends was stricken with toxic shock syndrome. She was urgently flown to Mayo Clinic, where I saw her body, swollen like a deer that had been dead for days, no facial features even visible, lying in a hospital bed with every muscle cavity in her body sliced open to drain the poison. It was a miracle she was still alive. I believe God placed me there for much of the 140-day stay to comfort and serve her parents.

My own physical issues have been enough to earn a chapter in a medical textbook! Two knee replacements, one hip replacement, a detached retina surgery, lower back laminectomy, removal of a fistula and multiple resections of my intestinal tract and perforated colon, arthroplasty of the carpometacarpal joint on my right hand, and cataract surgery on both eyes. And from my exposure in Vietnam to the toxin Agent Orange came many debilitating and disabling conditions including skin cancers, permanent loss of nerve activity below both knees greatly impeding my mobility, loss of bone density resulting in several broken bones, and more.

Each of these experiences were accompanied by their own sense of loss, and pain, and suffering, and each has been in its own way traumatic. They all contribute to the significance of what follows in this book as I write, not motivated by a sense of duty, or sympathy, but from the reality of a shared experience that has made me who I am and what I feel. There is, above all, joy that comes from the opportunity to be a help and blessing to others, for the glory of Almighty God.

CHAPTER 2

Building a Life On a Solid Foundation

AS WE BEGIN OUR JOURNEY TOWARDS understanding and action, it is important to articulate some foundational principles upon which we can build a meaningful narrative.

In his Sermon on the Mount, Jesus Christ taught his first disciples much about how they would live their lives as the sons and servants of God. That sermon is recorded in Matthew chapters 5, 6, and 7. The conclusion emphasizes the importance of building a life on a solid foundation. Here is what the Lord said:

> *Therefore whosoever heareth these sayings of mine, and doeth them, I will liken him unto a wise man, which built his house upon a rock: And the rain descended, and the floods came, and the winds blew, and beat upon that house; and it fell not: for it*

was founded upon a rock. And every one that heareth these sayings of mine, and doeth them not, shall be likened unto a foolish man, which built his house upon the sand: And the rain descended, and the floods came, and the winds blew, and beat upon that house; and it fell: and great was the fall of it. And it came to pass, when Jesus had ended these sayings, the people were astonished at his doctrine: For he taught them as one having authority, and not as the scribes. Matthew 7:24-29

At the onset of any battle, or threat of war, a strategic approach must be determined. So it is with our topic here: we must begin with a principled foundation upon which to build, then determine a strategy, and then go to battle. In this context, our foundation is the Word of God, and our strategy is to trust and obey, learning the Word and living the Word. Learning and living is the battlefront where the disciples of Jesus Christ are engaged!

Salvation is Our Solid Foundation for Spiritual Life

At the outset we should acknowledge some foundational Truth we already know and embrace. The condition of all of mankind alive today is that they are either "in Christ and saved," or "in sin and lost." According to God's Word, there are no other positions. It is a black and white certainty with no grey areas!

Jesus declared in John 3:18 that all without Him are condemned:

> *He that believeth on him is not condemned:* **but he that believeth not is condemned already** [emphasis added], *because he hath not believed in the name of the only begotten Son of God.*

As Jesus clearly states, mankind is "condemned already." We will remain so until we are reconciled to God. If any refuse reconciliation with God, they will remain condemned. If they die in this state, they will be forever condemned, separated from God in a place of eternal torment made worse by the knowledge that they chose it.

The essential Truth is that there is no neutral position regarding our standing with God. It is vital to grasp that we appear before God as "already condemned" sinners in need of a Savior. The process of reconciliation with God begins when our views and behaviors are confronted with Bible Truth. Some describe this Truth as the "real reality." I love that concept! We must not make the mistake of considering God as imaginary or fictitious. God and His kingdom are the ultimate reality! Fantasy Land only exists at a Disney theme park and in our imagination.

When confrontation with God's Truth occurs, the Holy Spirit of God convinces the sinner's conscience of their sin in order to bring about conviction, and ultimately confession. Confession is agreement with God, it is not "informing" God that we have done something against Him. He already knows that! We are the ones who need a change of mind about what confession is. We must come to a place of agreement with God.

Once convinced of our wrong, or bad, or sinful behavior, we have the freedom to exercise our free will. We can choose to either reject God or to repent of our sin. Simply put, repentance is a recognition of wrongdoing, a change of mind or attitude about wrong views or behaviors, and a turning to God, embracing His righteousness. True repentance is driven by a "godly sorrow." (See 2 Corinthians 7:10). In a nutshell, we agree with God in sorrow and sincerity, desiring His forgiveness because we are now willing to change our behavior.

I like to think of repentance as the beginning of the transformation process. One author describes it like this:

> The Christian life is a life imbued with the supernatural power and authority of God. God is the God of salvation. We do not control God by saying magic words or attending church. Conversion is a heart-affair. Before we can come to Christ, we must empty ourselves of the false pride, blame-shifting, excuse-making, and self-deception that preoccupy our days and our relationships. Before we can come to Christ, we must come to ourselves. [1]

When sinners turn away from their sinfulness, and by faith place their hope for eternal salvation in the finished work of Jesus Christ (See Acts 20:21), the Holy Spirit of God "quickens" them—makes them spiritually alive. This passage from spiritual death to spiritual life is a new birth into the family of God. Where sinners were once spiritually dead in their trespasses and sins, they are now alive in Christ. (See Ephesians chapter 2).

Whenever a pastor, a counsellor, or a trusted friend begins the process of aiding someone who may be tormented by past traumas, it is very helpful to have the hurting person share their personal testimony of salvation as a reminder that they belong to Christ and enjoy new life by exercising faith in Christ. For the helper, such a testimony is an affirmation that the individual they are seeking to aid has indeed received spiritual life in Christ. Expecting spiritually dead people to understand and discern God's Word is an exercise in futility!

I found the following statement in a book about the journey from a life of bondage to faith in Christ quite interesting on the topic of spiritual understanding, as the author shared her testimony about a faithful Christian introducing her to Christ.

> "The Bible makes it clear that reason is not the front door of faith. It takes spiritual eyes to discern spiritual matters. But how do we develop spiritual eyes unless Christians engage the culture with those questions and paradigms of mindfulness out of which spiritual

logic flows? That's exactly what Ken's letter did for me—invited me to think in ways I hadn't before." [2]

Healing and reconciliation are initiated on the foundation of one's salvation when a new, living relationship with God is established and the spiritual journey begins!

Sanctification is Our Normal Christian Life Experience

Spiritual regeneration happens in the redeemed because of their repentance and faith, and they are set on a new course of growing in the grace and knowledge of the Lord Jesus Christ. For the rest of their time on Earth, there will be an ongoing battle in their soul between good and evil, righteousness and unrighteousness. The new believer will have to make daily (sometimes hourly) choices toward good and toward righteousness or suffer the consequences that sin brings. Our soul is secure in Christ, and guaranteed a home in heaven, but the quality of our life on earth will be dependent on our cooperation with God in the sanctifying process of God conforming us to the image of His Son.

Sanctification is no small matter since anti-God world philosophies, the wanton flesh, and the deceitful devil, are constantly on attack to drag us down to a place of discouragement and defeat. If these anti-God opponents succeed, our ability to glorify God in the way we live is greatly hindered and in some cases rendered totally ineffective.

Reconciliation with God requires confession by the

sinner that prompts forgiveness from God. We must accept His forgiveness. This step is every bit as important as seeking forgiveness in the first place. Reconciliation is like a contract that allows us to move forward in our relationship with God, and with others, instead of being bogged down by the effects of our sin.

To help us solidify our foundation, we should also consider Christ's great call to discipleship. (Disciples are "adherents;" those who follow another's teachings). The call from Jesus is recorded after a series of parables about how one responds to opportunity: going through the motions without fulfilling the real purpose is pointless. Salt that loses its saltiness is of no value!

And then we read this:

*And there went great multitudes with him: and he turned, and said unto them, "If any man come to me, and hate not his father, and mother, and wife, and children, and brethren, and sisters, yea, and his own life also, **he cannot be my disciple**. And whosoever doth not bear his cross, and come after me, **cannot be my disciple**. For which of you, intending to build a tower, sitteth not down first, and counteth the cost, whether he have sufficient to finish it? Lest haply, after he hath laid the foundation, and is not able to finish it, all that behold it begin to mock him, saying, 'This man began to build, and was not able to finish.' Or what king, going to make war against another king, sitteth not down first, and consulteth whether he be able with ten thousand to meet him that cometh against him with* *twenty thousand? Or else, while the other is yet a great way off, he sendeth an ambassage, and desireth conditions of peace. So likewise, whosoever he be of you that forsaketh not all that he hath,* **he cannot be my disciple.***"* (Luke 14:25-33, emphasis added)

In this great call to discipleship, we see three tests in the form of emphatic statements. First, the disciple must have **a supreme love for Jesus Christ.** All other loves are like "hatred" in comparison. This teaches us that love of self can keep us from fully loving Christ. Jesus says, if you are not willing to let me be more important than any other relationship, you cannot be my disciple! Loving Jesus is not only an opportunity; it is a definite choice!

That leads to the second test: **complete submission to Christ is a requirement** (verse 27). This is more than self-denial; it is deliberately choosing the self-sacrificial life of the Cross, even to the point of bearing its shame and reproach. The question from Jesus is clear—are you willing to let Him be more important than any other plan or priority? Something in your life will always be "first." What have you placed at that point of priority?

The third test is closely related to the previous challenge: **will we spend our life following Christ?** It means we must learn the character of Christ and obey His commands. The question from Jesus is unequivocal: "Will my way always be your way?"

To be sure, these are not easy challenges! But look at the

illustrations the Lord uses. In verses 28-30 of Luke 14 His message is: ***"Plan before you build."*** If you don't plan, there are consequences—failure to complete the building, and mocking from those who observe your failure.

In verses 31-32, the message is: ***"Plan before you battle."*** Once again, if you don't plan, there are consequences. In this case, there may be a financial disaster ahead.

The Lord expects us to "**think**" (to plan); and then "**act**" (work). Notice that both steps are proactive exercises of personal will. If I were to find myself stuck in the mud, it would not be helpful to remain there complaining that I am stuck. I would need to make an action plan to free myself, and then implement the plan.

Life should be lived in much the same way. As we make progress on our journey, we will be faced with adversaries and adversities. This is simple reality! We must recognize that challenges are part of our growth process. The Apostle Peter exhorted believers in his day to "*grow in grace* (the enablement of God), *and in the knowledge of our Lord and Savior Jesus Christ.*" (2 Peter 3:18a.) Note that the text points us to Christ, who will lead us and teach us and strengthen us on our journey. For His work in us to be effective we must do more than just come to Him for help—we must submit wholly to Him for *life*.

Submission is the Way to Go

A study in the book of Matthew shows how Jesus began his

earthly ministry, establishing patterns to guide both those who seek help, and those who offer it. Matthew chapter one introduces the purpose and motivation for Jesus' ministry: He came to seek and to save the lost!

The beginning of His public ministry is described in Matthew chapter four (emphasis added):

> *And Jesus went about all Galilee, teaching in their synagogues, and preaching the gospel of the kingdom, and healing all manner of sickness and all manner or disease among the people.* ***And his fame went throughout all Syria: and they brought unto him all sick people*** *that were taken with diverse diseases and torments, and those which were possessed with devils, and those which were lunatick, and those that had the palsy;* ***and he healed them.*** *And* ***there followed him great multitudes of people*** *from Galilee, and from Decapolis, and from Jerusalem, and from Judea, and from beyond Jordan.* (Matthew 4:23-25).

We learn from the text that His "fame" spread, raising the question: *For what was Jesus famous?* Was it His teaching prowess? Was it His pure doctrine? Was it the Gospel message? These aspects all contributed to His fame, but the complete answer lies in the description of people who were brought to him, and what they received from Him.

1. ***They brought "sick people."*** Lost sinners are broken spiritually. Often, as a result of their sin, they are also

broken physically and emotionally. The original Greek word for "sick" (kakōs) means *badly amiss* (physically or morally). "Amiss" could mean diseased, evil, grievously, miserably, sick, or sore.[3] In short, people who sought help from Jesus were broken, hurting souls!

2. ***Did they come because of what He said, or because of what He did?*** People in trouble are moved more by what we do than by what we say! Jesus healed them!

3. ***Why did "they" (their friends) bring them?*** Driven by compassion or care, they were motivated by the hope or prospect of healing for those in need. The message Jesus preached was relatable to their life experience; they did not think in terms of spiritual healing, but the way Jesus met physical needs opened the door to addressing spiritual needs.

4. ***Why did a great multitude follow Him?*** The text informs us: *"And there followed him great multitudes of people from Galilee, and from Decapolis, and from Jerusalem, and from Judaea, and from beyond Jordan."* The healing work of Jesus was attractive! His reputation was proclaimed by those who witnessed His work. But here we must note that the focus of Jesus was on redemption and restoration, not on self-promotion, or growing a movement, or changing the world. Attraction by the Holy Spirit for the Glory of God, or promotion by ambitious "evangelists", are very different motivations that may be identified by asking if the fruit of a ministry results from **working for** God, or from God **working in us?**

CHAPTER 3

Stories of Radical Transformation

AS WE MAKE OUR WAY ALONG THE PATHWAY OF LIFE, we may encounter unfavorable situations and circumstances. Sometimes we recognize that the "status quo" has no benefit and no appeal, and it's at that point we are open to the idea of change.

"Change" will likely mean leaving some things behind forever and embracing new things that have never been part of our life experience. This may require rigorous honesty, openness to new challenges, and a decisive resolve to embrace the new by accepting the possibility of radical transformation. I can assure you that radical transformation is possible! Mine began on the evening of January 21, 1980, when at the age of 31, I put my faith and trust in Jesus Christ as my Savior! While some consider change very difficult, in my case the benefit of embracing change in my life quickly overpowered any fear of its difficulty.

There are numerous examples of this kind of change found in the Gospels. One dramatic account is recorded in the Gospel of Mark, chapter 5, verses 1 to 20. Parallel passages are found in Matthew 8:28-34 and Luke 8:26-39.

Before we unpack this story about demonic possession and deliverance, we must highlight the fact that it is impossible for competing spirits to inhabit the same person. In other words, if you have received the Spirit of God by surrender to Jesus Christ as your Savior, this Biblical Truth applies (from 2 Corinthians 5:17)—*If any man be in Christ, he is a new creature* [a new creation!]: *old things are passed away; behold, all things are become new.*

Likewise, *God would make known what is the riches of the glory of this mystery among the Gentiles* [former unbelievers] *which is Christ in you, the hope of glory* (Colossians 1:27).

Jesus described this experience as being "born again" (John 3:3). He added, speaking of His ministry on earth, *God so loved the world, that He gave His only begotten Son, that whosoever believeth in Him should not perish, but have everlasting life.* (John 3:16).

The meaning is plain. Regardless of our former transgressions and sins, we are delivered from bondage to evil in any form, including demonic possession, when we surrender to Christ. Yet experiences ingrained from a life of sin or abuse will leave us vulnerable to demonic influence or oppression if we do not immerse in the Word of God as our new guiding Truth, and benefit from appropriate counselling by informed and dedicated fellow disciples of Christ. Old habits die hard! The purpose of this book is to show how those old habits can effectively be broken.

The Maniac of Gadara

The story follows a boat ride across the Sea of Galilee, where Jesus calmed a storm, and provides insight to the spiritual warfare that is a real feature of life in this present evil world. Jesus confronts a legion of demons who possessed a man often referred to in sermons as "The Maniac of Gadara." A "maniac" is a psychotic; a person who has trouble telling the difference between what's real and what's not. Webster defines a maniac as "someone who is or acts mentally unsound, especially: a person who behaves in a wildly foolish, reckless, or dangerous manner or a person who is extremely enthusiastic about something."

The person described in Mark's Gospel would certainly qualify as a maniac. Let's look at the passage:

> *And they came over unto the other side of the sea, into the country of the Gadarenes. And when he was come out of the ship, immediately there met him out of the tombs a man with an unclean spirit, Who had his dwelling among the tombs; and no man could bind him, no, not with chains: Because that he had often bound with fetters and chains, and the chains had been plucked asunder by him, and the fetters broken in pieces: neither could any man tame him. And always,*

night and day, he was in the mountains, and in the tombs, crying, and cutting himself with stones. But when he saw Jesus afar off, he ran and worshipped him, And cried with a loud voice, and said, What have I to do with thee, Jesus, thou Son of the most high God? I adjure thee by God, that thou torment me not.

For he said unto him, Come out of the man, thou unclean spirit. And he asked him, What is thy name? And he answered, saying, My name is Legion: for we are many. And he besought him much that he would not send them away out of the country.

Now there was there nigh unto the mountains a great herd of swine feeding. And all the devils besought him, saying, send us into the swine, that we may enter into them. And forthwith Jesus gave them leave. And the unclean spirits went out, and entered into the swine: and the herd ran violently down a steep place into the sea, (they were about two thousand;) and were choked in the sea.

And they that fed the swine fled, and told it in the city, and in the country. And they went out to see what it was that was done. And they come to Jesus, and see him that was possessed with the devil, and had the legion, sitting, and clothed, and in his right mind: and they were afraid. And they that saw it told them how it befell to him that was possessed with the devil, and also concerning the swine. And they began to pray him to depart out of their coasts.

And when he was come into the ship, he that had been possessed with the devil prayed him that he might be with him. Howbeit Jesus suffered him not, but saith unto him, Go home to thy friends, and tell them how great things the Lord hath done for thee, and hath had compassion on thee. And he departed, and began to publish in Decapolis how great things Jesus had done for him: and all men did marvel. (Mark 5:1-20).

This story provides a significant example of healing that may help us understand and address the modern-day problem we are considering. The following are important lessons for us:

- As we read the passage, the man and the demons seemed to manifest as a single unit. However, Jesus spoke directly to the demons when the man approached Him.

- As the story unfolds it becomes clear that the man was not in control of his life; demonic spirits were controlling him. Jesus understood that simply attempting to change the man's behavior without addressing the core spiritual issue would be a futile exercise.

- Until Jesus sent the demons away, the man made no rational actions or choices other than fleeing to Jesus for help. Lost people are drawn by God, to God (John 6:44 and 12:32). As sad as this may be, many resist the impulse. We all have a God-given free will to exercise as we choose. We must realize that evil influences can cause us to resist God and His love.

- Once the spiritual conflict was resolved in this case, the man of Gadara experienced a radical transformation that is a wonderful picture of God's original intent for mankind, to willingly submit to Him and worship Him.

A Terrible Life – Powerless Against Sin

The maniac had suffered bondage, agony, and misery. His daily experience was far beyond what we could likely imagine. There must have been days when death seemed a better option than living. His physical pain and mental anguish were obvious through his circumstance and behavior.

Yet he was somebody's son! A part of his tortured mind no doubt remembered a happier previous life. Perhaps he thought sometimes of his broken-hearted mother or a frustrated father, although the text does not mention them. He may have been someone's brother, or husband. He may have had children, or grandchildren, but if that was the case, the story indicates that he was no longer engaged in any meaningful relationships. He was exiled from society and seemed to bear no burden of personal responsibility, living like a soul-less beast of the field in the shadows of death!

He was physically alive, but spiritually dead, a wild man whom nobody could tame, living well outside of town, away from the common culture, not governed by a clock or a calendar. He inflicted physical pain and torture on his own body because the emotional agony of his constant plight was more than he could rationally bear. He was occasionally seen weeping and crying out, fostering a reputation that brought shame and fear to his former community. He had apparently lived this way for a long time; it was his chronic condition.

Perhaps one of the most difficult facts to absorb from his story is that the citizens who once formed his community dealt with his condition by rejecting him and isolating him. They simply looked the other way. He was none of their concern. They minded their own business. No man cared for his soul. How pitiful!

This is what true hopelessness looks like! The maniac of Gadara was powerless against sin, just like many in our world with whom we rub shoulders every day! If they are not introduced to the mercy and grace of God, these lost souls will die in their sin and experience an eternity of torment in a lake of fire.

A Lunatic Son

Another account of the Lord dealing with an afflicted soul is found in Matthew 17:14-21:

> *And when they were come to the multitude, there came to him a certain man, kneeling down to him, and saying, Lord, have mercy on my son: for he is a lunatick, and sore vexed: for ofttimes he falleth into the fire, and oft into the water. And I brought him to thy disciples, and they could not cure him.*
>
> *Then Jesus answered and said, O faithless and perverse generation, how long shall I be with you? how long shall I suffer you? bring him hither to me. And Jesus rebuked the devil; and he departed out of him: and the child was cured from that very hour.*

> *Then came the disciples to Jesus apart, and said,*
> *Why could not we cast him out?*
>
> *And Jesus said unto them, Because of your unbelief: for verily I*
> *say unto you, If ye have faith as a grain of mustard seed, ye shall*
> *say unto this mountain, Remove hence to yonder place; and it*
> *shall remove; and nothing shall be impossible unto you.*
> *Howbeit this kind goeth not out but by prayer and fasting.*
> (Matthew 17:14-21).

How sad! This anguished father, desperate for help with a troubled son, brings him to the disciples, hoping for relief and deliverance. They couldn't help him! But Jesus could! Can you imagine the disciple's frustration? They asked Jesus why they were unable to cure the boy.

The Lord's answer must have been humiliating. Jesus said it was because of their "unbelief." They were faithless and perverse because they did not engage God and His power to address the issues. What an incredible lesson to learn.

The Transforming Power of Christ

Clearly, the issue of mental illness is not foreign to the Scriptures, and it is equally clear from the Gospel narrative that dealing with it—and with illness in general—should not be left exclusively to the medical community. While Jesus did not deny the need for medical professionals to help sick or emotionally injured people, He certainly communicated that He is a vital component of treatment for them. There are few challenges in life that demand more dependence on faith in God than physical or mental disabilities!

With that in mind, we will complete this chapter by considering in greater detail the radical transforming power of Christ and the Gospel. Scripture plainly offers Jesus Christ as the answer to the destructive power of sin and our consequent alienation from God. Consider the following:

- *For I am not ashamed of the gospel of Christ,* **for it** *[the Gospel of Christ]* **is the power of God to salvation** *for everyone who believes, for the Jew first and also for the Greek.* (Romans 1:16. Emphasis added).
- *For the Son of man is come* **to seek and to save that which was lost.** (Luke 19:10. Emphasis added).
- *And she will bring forth a Son, and you shall call His name JESUS,* **for He will save His people from their sins.** (Matthew 1:21. Emphasis added).

The Greek word for "save" in Matthew 1:21 means to *deliver* or *protect* (literally or figuratively): **heal, preserve, save** (self), do well, be (make) whole.[4] This is not just forgiveness! It is deliverance, the first step in transformation!

The evidence and experiences of transformed lives in those whom Jesus touched are clearly visible in Scripture. In the case of the Maniac of Gadara, pay close attention to the command Jesus gave him at the end of their encounter, to go back to his community and testify, to give witness of the work of God accomplished in his own life. In so doing, the transformation in the man would speak louder than words! Several elements of that change would be clearly apparent.

Peace

Instead of being distant, destructive, and dreadful in his behavior, the former maniac is seen sitting at the feet of Jesus, clothed, and in his right mind. God gave that peace! The Apostle Paul reminds us of our helpless estate without Christ.

> *For when we were still **without strength**, in due time Christ died for the ungodly. For scarcely for a righteous man will one die; yet perhaps for a good man someone would even dare to die. But God demonstrates His own love toward us, in that while we were still sinners, Christ died for us. Much more then, having now been justified by His blood, we shall be saved from wrath through Him.* (Romans 5:6-9 NKJV. Emphasis added).

Peace is found in a person! Not in religion, but in a personal relationship with our Savior. The transforming power of Christ brings peace to a troubled, broken soul.

Desire

The maniac's desire had been changed. He now wanted nothing more than to remain in the presence of Jesus, the one who brought relief, who delivered him from his daily hell! Walking with the Lord would be a delight, not just a duty.

A related incident is described in the Gospel of John, chapter 6, when many who heard Christ's teaching turned away because what they heard challenged their belief. The Lord asked his closest followers if they would also abandon Him. Peter responded with a profound statement: "***Lord,*** *to whom shall we go? You have the words of eternal life.*" (John 6:68).

Responses are still the same today. When someone invests faith and trust in Jesus Christ there follows an immediate desire to associate with fellow believers. Others less committed turn away when Bible teaching seems too invasive or demanding, challenging their own desires. Clearly, a desire to be with Jesus and stick close to others who love Him is an indication of intense gratitude that flows from genuine faith. Such desire is the fruit of true repentance and radical transformation.

Obedience

When told to go and tell his community about the great things God had done for him, the former maniac obeyed! He understood "the will of God" and would do it! This is a clear demonstration of true conversion to Christ. The Christian life is simple at its core: **Trust and Obey!** Faith in Christ may be defined as taking God at His word and acting accordingly. We are saved by faith, and we are to live by faith, by the Word of God. It is God's way. Only He has the structure of success for our lives, and it is found in the Bible.

For the man from Gadara overcoming any fear of change resulted in immense blessing! And for the father and the lunatic son, change was a tremendous blessing. Both embraced the work of God and benefitted from it.

If we, as a ministry, view reaching people with the Gospel as a method for growing our ministry, our purpose is a bit skewed! We reach people because they are lost and separated from our Saviour. They are dead in trespasses and sin. Once saved, we minister to them for their spiritual growth in their new life in Christ. It is a believer who is experiencing healing and growing that tells others in their circle of influence of the power of God at work in their lives. They "witness" to others in need of the healing power of God in their own lives. Their witness is attractive to those who are suffering the pain and effects of sin, whether lost or saved. This attraction is far different philosophically from church growth promotions.

This is the same approach Jesus took with the maniac from Gadara after he was delivered. See Mark 5:18-20.

CHAPTER 4

The Vast Scope of Mental Illness: Its Wounds and Scars

SOMETIMES THE RIPPLING EFFECTS OF SIN AND THE trauma of life experience are so great that spiritual growth and relationship building for the redeemed sinner is painfully slow. The sinner's brokenness impacts body, soul, and spirit! The inner sickness, and hurt, and disability cries out for healing.

Physical and Moral Wounds

We usually think of wounds as physical injuries to the body, such as cuts, bruises, burns, or broken bones. A moral wound is different. It is deep emotional or psychological harm caused by actions or experiences that violate personal ethics, values, and sense of right or wrong. Feelings of guilt, shame, and betrayal may arise from witnessing or participating in, or being a victim of, morally distressing events in wartime, or physical or sexual abuse, or experiences creating ethical dilemmas that manifest as depression, anxiety, and doubts about the meaning of life. Long-term emotional suffering that arises as a consequence is a component of PTSD.

The word "mental" simply means "relating to the mind." [5] Illness there can be deeply painful. Moreover, moral wounds usually take longer to heal and can leave lasting emotional scars.

It is important to understand that physical injuries are usually the result of immediate events, but moral or mental wounds typically result from debilitating and often traumatic events or exposures over prolonged periods of time. This is why it is more difficult to identify or even acknowledge a moral wound, and explains why sufferers are often resistant to treatment that requires both emotional and psychological healing that may include therapy, moral reconciliation, and/or spiritual support.

Using a medical analogy related to the treatment of physical injury, we could categorize the necessary steps required to bring about inner healing in the following way:

1.   Triage – Stop the "bleeding" or start the "breathing" to stabilize the sufferer before treatment of the underlying problem can commence. Apply "spiritual first aid" in the form of recognition and acceptance that sparks hope and a cooperative attitude.

2.   Treatment – Identify the wounds, whether emotional, moral or spiritual and determine a course of action

to begin the healing process. The goal is to achieve a safe return to a normal condition of good inner health.

3. Therapy – Ongoing care in the form of emotional support, prayer, teaching and application of appropriate biblical principles. This step demands the attention of an experienced Christian counsellor and broader support from the close Christian community, the Body of Christ.

The ultimate goal is deliverance from an oppressive inner condition and restoration to a normal Christian life removed from the chaos of the past and free to develop a deeply satisfying relationship with God.

Understanding Trauma

"Heartbreak" is a word often used without considering the full implication of its meaning or its cause, or appreciating the fact that true "heartbreak" can permanently alter the trajectory of a human life and its capacity for enjoying simple human pleasures. In a Christian context a more appropriate term for heartbreak would be a "broken soul," that is, a personal identity so damaged by trauma that it is almost impossible to fully *comprehend with all saints what is the breadth, and length, and depth, and height; and to know the love of Christ, which passeth knowledge, that ye might be filled with all the fulness of God.* (Ephesians 3:18-19).

A friend of mine, a trauma counselor, explained trauma this way:

"It occurs when an event or experience overwhelms our mind or body to the degree that we cannot respond in the usual fight or flight capacity. In this instance our mind and body completely shut down, ceasing to function according to their ability, until the actual or perceived danger has passed."

My friend added that two things occur when the mind and body shut down. First, the event or experience is not processed through the cortex part of our brain (the thinking, logical part) but remains trapped and unprocessed in the limbic part of the brain (the part based on emotions, which has no concept of time).

Secondly, our survival responses are trapped and unable to be cycled out through our natural fight or flight mechanism. The normal response when we are in a state of great fear, for example, is for our central nervous system to be loaded with stress hormones that prepare us for fight, or flight. If that natural cycle is hampered by dissociation ("zoning out"), our bodily responses remain activated, with no relief.

This condition is characterized by rapid heart and respiratory rate, increased blood pressure, sweating, changes in our intestinal tract, nausea, or anxiousness, to name a few responses. If there is no relief the condition becomes so overwhelming, day after day, that individuals will do anything to dampen the feelings that come with the state of hypervigilance, impending doom, and chronic fear. The typical next step is to fall back on unhealthy coping mechanisms and addictions. When the body finds something that will relieve the chronic state of fear and activation, the mind will do anything to replicate that relief, pursuing it at all costs.

Processing Trauma and Grief

God gave us a will that we must exercise to obey Him. Obedience means that we follow God's path by applying biblical principles designed to grow our spiritual strength and weaken our old nature, including destructive old habits. God will not force His way upon us—every right choice we make is voluntary. This means that when we learn what to do, we should do it without expecting any intervention from God until we complete the task. Spiritual blessings always come after we do right, not before it!

Intentional and persistent Bible study, preferably guided by a Christian well-grounded in his faith, is essential to Learn from our past, Look toward our future, and Live our life today! Living in the past is not helpful. Learn from it and move on!

CHAPTER 5

The Recognition of Mental Illness

THE CAUSES OF MENTAL ILLNESS ARE MANY. SOME of the more commonly recognized causes include traumatic exposure to violence; physical, verbal, or sexual abuse; persistent rejection from, or neglect by those closest to us; chemical dependency and other addictions; grief or loss; excessive stress; lifestyle choices and even genetics. The brain, our mind and our response to traumatic events or circumstances is the battleground.

Those experiencing mental illness may wonder if their mental faculties have been short-circuited to the point where reasoning and logic skills are affected. They may conclude that their thinking process needs fixing, or that their circumstances need to change. They are unsure of what is cause, and what is effect.

Circumstances are usually the cause of happiness or

unhappiness. But Scripture is clear that if our thinking aligns with God's precepts as outlined and illustrated in His Word (The Beatitudes are a powerful example, particularly Matthew 5:11-12), it is possible to experience peace and joy regardless of our circumstances!

The Destructive Stigma, "Who Is At Fault?"

A misunderstanding of the causes of mental illness gives rise to a destructive stigma attaching to the mentally ill. In extreme cases, sufferers may be seen as lazy, or weak, lacking the willpower to overcome their adversity. The observers are thinking, "What did they do?" or "Who did what that brought this on?" The underlying principle is that of judgment for wrong behavior.

There are lessons to be learned from the story of Jesus healing a man born blind (John 9:1-5):

> *And as Jesus passed by, he saw a man which was blind from his birth. And his disciples asked him, saying, Master, **who did sin**, this man, or his parents, that he was born blind? Jesus answered, **Neither hath this man sinned, nor his parents**: that the works of God should be made manifest in him. I must work the works of him that sent me, while it is day: the night cometh, when no man can work. As long as I am in the world, I am the light of the world.* (Emphasis added).

While the story speaks of a physical condition, the same principle may apply to a mental state. Consider the following:

- The blind man was not guilty—he was born with a condition that caused him much distress, but Jesus' disciples immediately presumed to cast blame, in essence asking, "Who's at fault here?"

- The answer that Jesus gives is uncomfortable to consider because He invites us to step back from the problem and look up! Our Creator God had a purpose in this case: "manifesting His work!" (verse 3). This is not true in every case of suffering or adversity, but we should learn from this story to be cautious in assigning blame or presuming to know the Will of God. It is far more important that we respond with compassion and present God's mercy and grace while seeking His Wisdom in His Word to guide us further in assisting a fellow soul in need.

- The ultimate remedy for every negative human condition is simply to walk with the Lord and listen to His voice, for it is then that this powerful statement in Romans 8:28 applies in every circumstance: *We know that all things work together for good to them that love God, to them who are the called according to his purpose.*

As I author this book, equipped with decades of learning through study and personal experience, a recurring thought comes to mind: Why do we so often fail to hear and respond to the cry of the hurting for help within the Christian community? I wonder if we are so busy with programs and activities that we don't stop to hear or recognize the cries of those in our midst who are desperate for relief and healing from mental and emotional infirmity. If we cannot hear them, we will not be stirred by compassion to help them! How long might it be before the unheard cry becomes a life-threatening crisis?

Mental Illness and the Christian Community

Perhaps we are deaf to those cries because we have not taken on board the possibility of mental health infirmity among Christians? Yet it is not something new or exclusive to our time and place. To validate this assertion, I offer the following comments from other scholars and ministers of God's Word, regarding mental illness in the ministry!

Charles Spurgeon

Spurgeon suffered from intense, long-term depression! The great evangelist made frequent references to his ailment in his sermons. Here are some examples that I have categorized under appropriate headings.

Spurgeon's Depression and Suicidal Thoughts
From "**Israel's God and God's Israel.**"

> "I suppose that some brethren neither have much elevation or depression. I could almost wish to share their peaceful life. For I am much tossed up and down,

and although my joy is greater than the most of men, my depression of spirit is such as few can have an idea of."

"I could say with Job, 'My soul chooseth strangling rather than life' [Job 7:15]. I could readily enough have laid violent hands upon myself, to escape from my misery of spirit."

"I wonder every day that there are not more suicides, considering the troubles of this life."

Depression and Anxiety as Medical Problems, not Sins
In a sermon called "**The Fear of Death**," and another, "**Night and Jesus Not There**."

"There are certain forms of disease which so affect the brain and whole nervous system that depression is a melancholy symptom of the disease."

"I would not blame all those who are much given to fear, for in some it is rather their disease than their sin, and more their misfortune than their fault."

It must be stressed that the greatest evangelical preacher of the 19th century designated fear as a disease and not a sin, that it is "misfortune" more than "fault"!

The Sudden, Inexplicable Onset of Mental Illness
From his sermon, "**The Saddest Cry of the Cross**."

"Quite involuntarily, unhappiness of mind, depression of spirit, and sorrow of heart will come upon you. You may be without any real reason for grief and yet may become among the most unhappy of men."

From "**Night and Jesus not there.**"

"There is a kind of mental darkness, in which you are disturbed, perplexed, worried, troubled – not, perhaps, about anything tangible."

The Folly of Judging Those With Mental Health Problems
From "**Man Unknown To Man.**"

"Especially judge not the sons and daughters of sorrow. Allow no ungenerous suspicions of the afflicted, the poor, and the despondent.

Do not hastily say they ought to be more brave and exhibit a greater faith. Ask not 'why are they so nervous and so absurdly fearful?' No… I beseech you, remember that you understand not your fellow man."

From his sermon, "**The Saddest Cry From the Cross**."

"Strong-minded people are very apt to be hard upon nervous folk and to speak harshly to people who are very depressed in spirit, saying 'really, you ought to rouse yourself out of that state'."

The sad part about all the above is that we do not seem to have progressed much since Spurgeon's time in our response to the ailment of mental stress and mental wounds.

The Psalm Writer

An Old Testament Psalmist recognized spiritual depression when he wrote:

> [To the chief Musician, Maschil, for the sons of Korah.] *As the hart panteth after the water brooks, so panteth my soul after thee, O God. My soul thirsteth for God, for the living God: when shall I come and appear before God? My tears have been my meat day and night, while they continually say unto me, Where is thy God? When I remember these things, I pour out my soul in me: for I had gone with the multitude, I went with them to the house of God, with the voice of joy and praise, with a multitude that kept holyday. Why art thou cast down, O my soul? and why art thou disquieted in me? hope thou in God: for I shall yet praise him for the help of his countenance. O my God, my soul is cast down within me: therefore will I remember thee from the land of Jordan, and of the Hermonites, from the hill Mizar. Deep calleth unto deep at the noise of thy waterspouts: all thy waves and thy billows are gone over me. Yet the LORD will command his lovingkindness in the daytime, and in the night his song shall be with me, and my prayer unto the God of my life. I will say unto God my rock, Why hast thou forgotten me? why go I mourning because of the oppression of the enemy? As with a sword in my bones, mine enemies reproach me; while they say daily unto me, Where is thy God?* **Why art thou cast down, O my**

soul? and why art thou disquieted within me? *hope thou in God:* for I shall yet praise him, *who is the health of my countenance*, and my God. (Psalm 42:1-11. Emphasis added)

David Martyn-Lloyd Jones

Martyn-Lloyd Jones, a Welsh Congregationalist minister and medical doctor who ministered in the mid-1900's and was for 30 years the minister at Westminster Chapel in London, addressed mental health issues in his classic book, *Spiritual Depression: Its Causes and Cures.* The book summary reads:

> This enduring collection of twenty-one sermons by D. Martyn-Jones, each originally delivered at Westminster Chapel in London, carefully and compassionately analyzes an undeniable feature of modern society from which Christians have not escaped—spiritual depression.
>
> "Christian people," writes Lloyd-Jones, "too often seem to be perpetually in the doldrums and too often give this appearance of unhappiness and of lack of freedom and absence of joy. There is no question at all but that this is the main reason why large numbers of people have ceased to be interested in Christianity."
>
> Believing that Christian joy was one of the most potent factors in the spread of Christianity in the early centuries, Lloyd-Jones not only lays bare the causes that have robbed many Christians of spiritual

vitality but also points the way to the cure that is found through the mind and spirit of Christ.[6]

Jones suggests that when dealing with spiritual depression one begins with the issue of temperament. We all have one! And it will greatly influence our Christian experience. It seems to me that our temperament flows out of our psyche and is part of how God shaped us. As Christians, we are not all identical, and we were never intended to be. While general principles of treatment may apply to all, there will be need for some more focused and individualized approaches and methods for each person.

Lloyd-Jones added:

"There are so-called introverts and extroverts. There is a type of person who is generally looking inwards and the type of person who is always looking outwards and it is of the greatest importance that we should realize not only that we belong to one or the other of these two groups, but furthermore that this condition of spiritual depression tends to affect the one more than the other. [7]

We could cite other examples of ministers of God's Word who have identified and addressed mental health issues in Christians. The important point I want to make is that we are not facing a new problem. Mental illness in some form or other has been present during the entire history of mankind. Church leaders must recognize this if we are to be a help and blessing to those who suffer silently in our midst.

A Perspective on Mental Illness – Public and Private

Our prayer lists are populated with requests for healing from physical sickness. There are some requests for spiritual healing through salvation or the recovery of backsliders. That takes care of the outwardly sick and the lost and the backslidden, but how many requests do we see for "soul-sickness"? Could it be that some, perhaps many, or even most of the so-called "unspoken prayer requests" are for healing in this area?

It is as if we treat soul-sickness like the leprosy of the Old Testament by isolating it and staying clear of those stricken with it. Surely it is time to openly address this problem and develop the means to deal with it in our Bible-believing churches.

CHAPTER 6

Scriptural Admonitions to Discipline the Mind

THERE ARE MANY ENCOURAGEMENTS AND exhortations in Scripture regarding our thinking processes and how they relate to our behavior. We might say that God's Word is a filtration system for the mind, exhorting us to take personal responsibility for our thoughts, both as to our thought processes and the things we think about. We should be intentional in the way we think; but it is easier said than done!

Competing Voices

Many voices seek to influence us. Friends, family, school or the workplace, and the surrounding culture apply constant pressure. Movies, television, the internet and music have a massive impact on the way we think, what we believe, and how we behave. All these inputs impinge on our individuality to the point that it may be difficult to know what we should think, and if we are thinking our own thoughts or the thoughts of others. Some voices appeal to our intellect while others seek to influence our emotions.

A family friend named Elouise, who was in long-term recovery and worked briefly at our addiction treatment facility while maintaining her 12-step program, would often refer to "the little bitty shitty committee" that always had something to say to her; the negative voices in her mind that were constantly trying to draw her back into her old ways. It was an ongoing battle to turn the voices away. Most people in recovery from addiction have an experience like the old cartoon where the main character's will is under assault. On one shoulder is a little angel and on the other a little red devil with a pitchfork in hand. The angel encourages the character to do right, and the devil is always egging him on to do wrong!

While the cartoon made for good entertainment, the reality is an ongoing battle for control of the mind. The Old Testament prophet offered great encouragement towards winning the battle when he wrote: *"Thou wilt keep him in perfect peace, whose mind is stayed on thee: because he trusteth in thee."* (Isaiah 26:3). This is an incredible truth that too few are willing to believe. It seems too simplistic. It probably comes with strings attached! Scripture acknowledges these doubts when it declares that without faith it is impossible to please God—*"for he that cometh to God must believe that he is, and that he is a rewarder of them that diligently seek him."* (Hebrews 11:6).

How We Discipline Our Minds, Our Thinking Processes and Thought Patterns

Psychology is a science, which means that there are specific methods for asking questions, gathering data, and answering questions related to the human psyche. The process is not complicated, although the application may be. In a Christian context it is simple: To overcome psychological conflict, arm yourself with Truth!

Love the Truth – Recognize the Truth is what God presents to us because He has determined what is best for us. Give yourself to it. Pursue it! Stand by the Truth and with the Truth. Make it your constant companion and the master of your mind! When you love the Truth, you will be quick to recognize when it is under attack.

Learn the Truth – Make the most of every opportunity to learn God's Word. This includes personal reading and study and submitting to good, solid Bible teaching as often as possible. Being a faithful church attender is not primarily for the benefit of the church, but for your benefit. In a Christ-centered church you will find God-ordained servants to help you learn the Truth. When you know the real thing, you will be able to recognize the counterfeit.

Live the Truth – Put into practice what God teaches you through His Word and by His servants. Trust God and obey Him. Hard to believe as it is, when you submit to God you become His personal project. The Bible depicts Him as the potter, and you as the clay.

Consider these informative passages of Scripture:

*Be sober, be vigilant; because your adversary the devil, as a roaring lion, walketh about, seeking whom he may devour: Whom resist steadfast **in the faith**,* (definite article is used meaning "the faith" is the whole body of Truth, God's Word) *knowing that the same afflictions are accomplished in your brethren that are in the world.* (1 Peter 5:8-9)

See then that ye walk circumspectly, not as fools, but as wise, redeeming the time, because the days are evil. Wherefore be ye not unwise, but understanding what the will of the Lord is. (Ephesians 5:15-17).

And be not drunk with wine, wherein is excess; but be filled with the Spirit; speaking to yourselves in psalms and hymns and spiritual songs, singing and making melody in your heart to the Lord; giving thanks always for all things unto God and the Father in the name of our Lord Jesus Christ; (Ephesians 5:18-20).

It will serve you well to recognize that we are conditioned to be undisciplined in our thought life. The mindset of the culture regarding the priority of our thinking is exposed in the phrase, "Amusement Park." It is perfectly captured in the word "amusement" itself! The root word of amusement is "muse," which means "to think." The prefix "a" added to the root means "No." Together we get a word meaning "no think!" This is exactly what the enemy of our souls wants to achieve, in line with the old proverb: "An idle mind is the devil's playground."

Taking our little word study a step further, when the suffix "ment" is added to the word "amuse" we get "amusement," which literally means "no think action"! But God did not design mankind for a life of passive amusement. He designed us for a lifetime of active service, fellowship, and worship.

Self-Discipline requires making and executing a plan to move us in a positive direction away from the negative conditions or circumstances that haunt our thinking. Intentionally creating a structured thinking environment is an important part of addiction treatment programs. Failure to do this often leads to relapse within a short period of time. The proper environment is also a vital part of the healing process for a broken soul. Intent and structure are critical elements of our thinking discipline that will foster the healing we desire.

Think on These Things

Take a look at a significant passage of Scripture regarding our minds and how to think:

> *Rejoice in the Lord alway: and again I say, Rejoice. Let your moderation* [appropriateness, patience] *be known unto all men. The Lord is at hand. Be careful for nothing* [don't be anxious]*; but in everything by prayer and supplication with thanksgiving let your requests be made known unto God.* [Do you see structure and intent here?] *And the peace of God,*

which passeth all understanding, shall keep your hearts and minds through Christ Jesus. Finally, brethren, whatsoever things are true, whatsoever things are honest, whatsoever things are just, whatsoever things are pure, whatsoever things are lovely, whatsoever things are of good report; if there be any virtue, and if there be any praise, **think on these things**. *Those things, which ye have both learned, and received, and heard, and seen in me,* **do**: *and* **the God of peace shall be with you.** (Philippians 4:1-9. Emphasis added).

The exhortation by the Apostle Paul highlights an important truth that impacts all of us every day: We have the ability to control what we think, and then, by the grace of God, to do the positive things we think about! Trust and obey, and the result will be an experience of the peace of God as He sets our soul at ease!

Again, it requires mind discipline! *"Think on these things"* (vs 8) is an instruction to be intentional about what is in our mind at all times. Implied in the verse is that we could intentionally choose to think about other things. Earlier in the quoted passage we read: *"let this mind be in you which was also in Christ Jesus"* (2:5). The implication is that we have control over our thought processes and the content of our thoughts. We must exercise discipline!

Lest we see this as an overwhelming task, Paul on another occasion told the Corinthian church, *"We have the mind of Christ,"* (1 Corinthians 2:15). As believers in

Christ, we have the Holy Spirit living in us to help us understand and apply the revealed Word of God. Simply put, if we don't control our mind, our mind will control us! The natural habitual tendency of our minds is toward that which is characteristic of opposition to God. Here is how Paul described the minds of those who have not submitted to God:

> *This I say therefore, and testify in the Lord, that ye henceforth walk not as other Gentiles walk, in the vanity of their mind, having the understanding darkened, being alienated from the life of God through the ignorance that is in them, because of the blindness of their heart: who being past feeling have given themselves over unto lasciviousness* [indecency], *to work all uncleanness with greediness.* (Ephesians 4:17-19).

The resisters of God's grace are empty-minded, void of understanding, and godless. The result is ignorance and the absence of God. It leads to a guilt-free indulgence of sin, and a deepening bondage as the unregenerate person resists the love of God.

Paul's exhortation boils down to this; discipline your mind! Following natural impulses instead of trusting and obeying God is a prescription for trouble. The principle of sowing and reaping plays a role here! Garbage in, Garbage out!

From the above passage in Philippians 4:1-9, let's

consider further what God wants us to think about as we analyze the original Greek words. We are to think about things that are:

- **True =** alēthēs (al-ay-thace, true, not concealing)[8] Focus thinking on the Truth; on true things! Do not be open to listen to that which is not true – gossip, slander, lies, etc. Focus becomes easier when we fill our heart and mind with God's Word.

- **Honest =** semnos (sem-nos, venerable, honorable, grave, honest).[9] Think about respectful and honorable things. Looking at the opposite of honorable includes things that are immoral, bad, corrupt, and deceptive. Honorable things elevate God.

- **Just =** dikaios (equitable in character or action, by implication innocent, holy, just, appropriate, righteous).[10] God is the one who determines and defines what is just. Our understanding of what is just is greatly enhanced when we learn from Scripture the commandments, statutes, and judgments of God. These give direction for life application of God's Truth.

- **Pure =** hagnos (properly clean, figuratively innocent, modest, perfect in the sense of being chaste, clean, pure).[11] Purity is maligned in this present age. Filth has become the modality of comedy and of everyday speech. It permeates radio, TV, the internet and common public discourse! Premarital sex is recreational for many, while purity is mocked. But a commitment to purity in God's culture makes that which is impure glaringly apparent and profoundly ugly!

- **Lovely =** prosphilēs (friendly towards, that is, acceptable, lovely).[12] The political environment marred by liberal and progressive thought has divided our society to the extent that people hate those whom they have never met, nor do they have any sort of interaction with them. This is in dramatic contrast to loving God and sharing His love with others. Jesus taught his first disciples this foundational truth, *"But I say unto you, Love your enemies, bless them that curse you, do good to them that hate you, and pray for them which despitefully use you, and persecute you;"* Matthew 5:44. Wrong thinking destroys wholesome, peaceful culture.
- **Good Report =** euphēmos (well-spoken of, reputable, of good report).[13] We have in our tongue the power to either encourage or to destroy. The choice is driven by the condition of our heart. Man is not the judge of others, rather his purpose is to testify of the work of God in his own life. Thinking like this produces good reports for others to hear.

Encouraged by the above examples from Scripture we should develop a strategic thinking plan for our life, to think biblically, to think honestly, to embrace the judgments of God in our thoughts. Purity and wholesomeness should filter our thinking. Gossip or criticism must not be allowed to highjack our thoughts.

Paul's Four Step Program from Romans Chapter 6

The Church at Philippi wasn't the only one where Paul addressed the thought process. He also wrote to the Church at Rome, and in his letter, he laid out what could be regarded as "the Christian 4-step program"—Know, Reckon, Yield, Grow!

Step One - KNOW: verses 1-10 – Paul reminds the believers about their position in Christ. We are no longer slaves to sin or the slave-master; rather we are now free to live a new life in Christ; a life that reflects God's glory.

A careful reading of this passage will reveal that there are several steps within the first step, indicating that it takes time to build our intellectual data bank about the ways of God and our power to walk in those ways. This in turn amplifies our need to submit to the ministry of a God-called pastor able to teach what it means to be a follower of Christ. Our appetite for learning from God's Word will grow, beginning with the "milk of the word," progressing on to "the bread of the Word," until we are eventually able to feast on the "meat of the Word." Through this process we will develop an insatiable appetite for God and His Word!

Step Two - RECKON: Verses 11-12 – Once we have gained knowledge and understanding from God's Word we will need to apply it to our lives. To "reckon" means to "treat accordingly." [14] We have learned what the Word says. We understand that the Word of God is the Will of God for us, and so we treat it as such, replacing our old way of thinking because we reckon that God's way is more reliable and effective than our own way. God is always working for our good and His glory. "*And we know that all things work together for good to them that love God, to them who are the called according to his purpose.*" (Romans 8:28).

I think we could say that the instructions in verses 1-12 are akin to "forming a new neural pathway," providing us with the teaching and encouragement to develop changes in our behavior. (See Chapter 9 for more information about neural pathways).

Step Three - YIELD: Verses 13-20 – Armed with our understanding and knowledge from God's Word, and being convinced by the indwelling Holy Spirit that these truths apply to us personally, we take the next step by yielding our life—our way of thinking and doing—to God and His ways. This is a choice we make based on our growing trust in God and our desire to obey Him. This is often referred to as our "surrender" or "consecration." We have trusted Christ for our salvation; now we look to Him as our Lord! Our will is subservient to His will. We live for Him; His cause; His purpose; His glory! Our life as a light now illuminates and magnifies Him, not us.

Step Four – GROW: Verses 21-23 – Here we experience the fruitfulness of resurrection life. By our progress through the first three steps, a new disciplined lifestyle emerges. We are engaged in discipleship, and the process of sanctification. God is conforming us to the image of His dear Son!

In this stage we willfully and intentionally establish a defense against the enemies of God and our enemies, which include the world, the flesh, and the devil (see Ephesians 2:1-3 and James 3:15), by putting on the whole armor of God and resisting the devil until he flees from us (Ephesians 6:10-18), all the while understanding that the respite may be temporary. We live recognizing that in the seasons of comfort there is an inherent risk of complacency making us vulnerable to future attacks. Unceasing diligence and discipline are the order of the day.

Proverbs 11:30 teaches us that *"The fruit of the righteous is a tree of life; and he that winneth souls is wise."* The word "life" in this verse speaks of "welfare and happiness in the king's presence – eternally." [15]

It is possible that this verse is speaking more of an outcome than a strategy or an agenda! A dramatically changed life enhances the testimony of one who is a witness to the grace and power of God in transforming His close followers. A righteous life, when observed, is a great tool in the hands of Almighty God to convince others to embark on the journey of hope and faith.

It is a wise man who understands the connection between a personal walk that matches a public witness.

Hide the Word in Your Heart

Paul's fourth step, Growing, cannot be fully achieved if we do not follow the admonition of Scripture to immerse in God's Word. Psalm 119, verse 11 declares: *"Thy Word have I hid in my heart, that I might not sin against thee."* Hiding God's Word in our heart means memorizing it so that at the precise moment of need it comes to mind, engaging our thinking process to influence our choices. The Apostle Paul told the Corinthians:

"There hath no temptation taken you but such as is common to man: but God is faithful, who will not suffer you to be tempted above that ye are able; but will with the temptation also make a way to escape, that ye may be able to bear it." (1 Corinthians 10:13)

Because we have learned and treasured God's Word, we have an arsenal at hand to resist temptations. The power of the mind is very significant! It must be trained to do right and to use the tools God has provided for our benefit.

The Psalms are Spirit-led thoughts from the minds of men, attracting many disciples to invest time in reading them and memorizing them. They expose the carnal thoughts of men and present the glorious reality of God. Here are examples:

"The law of the LORD is perfect, converting the soul: the testimony of the LORD is sure, making wise the simple. The statutes of the LORD are right, rejoicing the heart: the commandment of the LORD is pure, enlightening the eyes. The fear of the LORD is clean, enduring for ever: the judgments of the LORD are true and righteous altogether. More to be desired are they than gold, yea, than much fine gold: sweeter also than honey and the honeycomb. Moreover by them is thy servant

warned: and in keeping of them there is great reward. Who can understand his errors? cleanse thou me from secret faults. Keep back thy servant also from presumptuous sins; let them not have dominion over me: then shall I be upright, and I shall be innocent from the great transgression. Let the words of my mouth, and the meditation of my heart, be acceptable in thy sight, O LORD, my strength, and my redeemer." (Psalm 19:7-14)

Also consider the latter part of Psalm 104:

"O LORD, how manifold are thy works! in wisdom hast thou made them all: the earth is full of thy riches. So is this great and wide sea, wherein are things creeping innumerable, both small and great beasts. There go the ships: there is that leviathan, whom thou hast made to play therein. These wait all upon thee; that thou mayest give them their meat in due season. That thou givest them they gather: thou openest thine hand, they are filled with good. Thou hidest thy face, they are troubled: thou takest away their breath, they die, and return to their dust. Thou sendest forth thy spirit, they are created: and thou renewest the face of the earth. The glory of the LORD shall endure for ever: the LORD shall rejoice in his works. He looketh on the earth, and it trembleth: he toucheth the hills, and they smoke. I will sing unto the LORD as long as I live: I will sing praise to my God while I have my being. My meditation of him shall be sweet: I will be glad in the LORD." (Psalm 104:24-35)

David, in a Psalm about the Word of God declared: "*O how love I thy law! it is my meditation all the day.* (Psalm 119:97). Meditation is disciplined thinking. Intentional thinking!

Behavior Is Driven by Thought! Our Thinking Leads to Action

King Solomon wrote much about this truth to his son, recorded in the book of Wisdom.

> "*Eat thou not the bread of him that hath an evil eye, neither desire thou his dainty meats:* **For as he thinketh in his heart,** [figuratively, our mental being] *so is he: Eat and drink, saith he to thee; but his heart is not with thee. The morsel which thou hast eaten shalt thou vomit up, and lose thy sweet words.*" (Proverbs 23:6-8. Emphasis added).

Solomon exhorts his son to protect his heart/mind. "*Keep thy heart with all diligence; for out of it are the issues of life.*" (Proverbs 4:23). The father was teaching his son that our response to the issues of life will be determined by the condition of our heart at the moment we face the issue.

James, in his epistle makes the same point:

> "*Let no man say when he is tempted, I am tempted of God: for God cannot be tempted with evil, neither tempteth he any man: But every man is tempted, when he is drawn away of his own lust, and enticed. Then when lust hath conceived,*

[to find a beginning point] *it bringeth forth sin: and sin, when it is finished, bringeth forth death.*" (James 1:13-15).

Failure to discipline our mind makes us vulnerable to temptation. We need to be on guard because what we think about fuels our behavior! Consider this practical exercise: Examine your behavior this week and it may reveal some bad thought patterns that are robbing you of the joy and blessing that comes from rejecting temptations and following God!

CHAPTER 7

Church Ministry

THE CHURCH IS A PLACE WHERE SPIRITUALLY DAMAGED people find help and begin to heal. Some have greater needs than others, but all of us need healing that is part of spiritual growth.

Making Disciples

Every believer is a particular member of one body, a local church. *But now hath God set members every one of them in the body, as it hath pleased him.* (1 Corinthians 12:18).

In each local body of believers, the Lord calls some to be pastor-teachers and some to be evangelists. (The time of gifting and calling apostles and prophets is past now that we have the entirety of God's Word to enjoy).

But unto every one of us is given grace according to the measure of the gift of Christ. Wherefore he saith, When he ascended up on high, he led captivity captive, and gave gifts unto men. (Now that he ascended, what is it but that he also descended first into the lower parts of the earth? He that descended is the same also that ascended up far above all heavens, that he might fill all things.)

And he gave some, apostles; and some, prophets; **and some, evangelists: and some, pastors and teachers; For the perfecting of the saints, for the work of the ministry, for the edifying of the body of Christ:** *Till we all come in the unity of the faith, and of the knowledge of the Son of God, unto a perfect man, unto the measure of the stature of the fulness of Christ: That we henceforth be no more children, tossed to and fro, and carried about with every wind of doctrine, by the sleight of men, and cunning craftiness, whereby they lie in wait to deceive; But speaking the truth in love, may grow up into him in all things, which is the head, even Christ: From whom the whole body fitly joined together and compacted by that which every joint supplieth, according to the effectual working in the measure of every part, maketh increase of the body unto the edifying of itself in love.* (Ephesians 4:7-16. Emphasis added).

The role of pastor-teachers is to equip the saints (members of a local assembly) for the work of ministry—that is, to teach us how to serve inside and outside the church.

The members are brought to a place of maturity and unity in the faith (a common belief based on Truth). To "edify" means "the act of one who promotes another's growth in Christian wisdom, piety, holiness, and happiness."[16] It is a process designed to bring every believer to a mature relationship with Christ, as a disciple of Christ who is reconciled to his (or her) past, healed from past hurts and the damage caused by sin.

In other words, redemption opens the door for restoration, forgiveness and healing that puts an end to the inner conflict that hampers spiritual growth. In this context it is important to understand that hurting people don't learn well while the hurt continues! Ministers must be prepared to address the issues that interrupt the growing process.

Clearly, the goal in discipleship is not to mask problems but to help others shine their light! The psalmist expresses this thought very well: *Why art thou cast down, O my soul? and why art thou disquieted within me? hope thou in God: for I shall yet praise him, who is the health of my countenance, and my God.* (Psalm 42:11).

Overcoming the Stigma of Mental Illness

There is a stigma attached to mental illness, driven by ignorance that causes fear, shame, and denial. At the outset we must answer the question and deal with it accordingly: "If someone is not mentally well, are they mentally ill?" And in answering the question we must consider that the illness is not an expression of "self-will weakness" but of something deeper that sufferers cannot easily overcome. They can't "just get over it!" The sickness manifests as a behavioral problem that is a response to ingrained brain activity (see Chapter 9-Understanding Neural Pathways, for more technical detail), making it a soul condition in the same way that a broken leg is a physical condition.

Pastoral counsellors must understand this and proceed with care, compassion, and love in their ministry to those in need. This is especially true if the counsellor's limited expertise raises the question of referral to a psychologist, or psychiatrist. Would this feed the stigma and fuel more silent suffering? Is making a referral to a "shrink" a faithless exercise?

Reviewing This Ministry

How should we conduct this delicate yet important ministry? Are perception and reality in agreement? We may want to consider the following:

- A Church may revisit its understanding of "spiritual warfare," especially in the arena of demonic oppression—that is, when an individual is not possessed by a demon but is under sustained attack from a demonic source. Sadly, the common church "strategy" in this area is simple denial, where the possibility of demonic activity is not discussed or even recognized. How often have you seen someone oppressed with demonic influence and addressed it? Your answer may be revealing.

- It may be necessary to revisit the stated purpose of each area of ministry to see what message is being projected and perceived. Is the ministry ethos in the church one that projects the message, "We care about you," or is the message (whether real or perceived), "You must conform to us?" (In other words, We Care vs. You Should!).

- A foundational message in all areas of ministry should undergird the principle of confession and forgiveness as normal practice in Christian life; that is, when forgiveness is sought, it is both granted and received. It is an encouraging formula that brings sin out of darkness into God's light, especially when serious underlying issues prevail in the life of someone who has suffered emotional, physical, or spiritual trauma. Do you recognize those in the congregation who have suffered silently, received forgiveness, and now celebrate it by testifying of the work of God in their lives?

- Are we teaching the growth process of "Put Off-Be Renewed-Put On" that Paul lays out in Ephesians chapter 4, as the "normal course" of spiritual growth to overcome habitual sin and replace it with habitual righteousness? We do this, not to gain favor with God, but to glorify God! It is a sanctification process often articulated in the mental health community as "establishing a new neural pathway" that creates a "new way of thinking" or a "new perspective." This leads to a change in behavior; the fruit of our thinking.

- Part of "equipping the saints for the work of the

ministry" is teaching ministers to recognize and understand that the first cry for help from a hurting person is usually directed towards someone in whom they have a measure of trust or confidence. It is a cry that we should not ignore within the Body of Christ, with the further understanding that the minister's intent is not to be an enabler, but a helper. Rarely is that cry made to a pastor. How adept is the Body in hearing the cries?

- Make space for the facilitation of open testimony. When hurting people hear of others testifying of God's grace in overcoming personal difficulties, they are encouraged to seek help. Personal testimonies are powerful! In 12-step meetings, the testimonies are a major part of the process! One of the key slogans of Alcoholics Anonymous is *"Together they shared their experience, strength and hope."* Such sharing is facilitated where the environment is safe and comfortable, and where the culture is obvious that it is not only okay, but it is normal to be vulnerable and transparent.

- In my personal experience, the Twelve-Step program embraced by alcoholics and addicts helps one to move away from selfish isolation and towards selfless service, and even sacrificial service! The biblical process of disciple-making sets that same pattern. God saves a selfish, sin-driven person to enter a process of sanctification that will ultimately conform the sinner to the image of Christ who declared, *"Not my will, but thy will be done.*" It is this process that makes the mentally ill, mentally well! Much of the healing takes place in the soul, that is, in the realm of intellect, emotions, and will. Those helping the broken soul must be patient as this is a process that takes time. Like every other member of a church body, the Holy Spirit is at work. He knows exactly what each of us needs at the present time. We must not let our expectations define progress. God is at work, and we must trust Him.

Develop a Pastoral Culture in the Church

It seems that in any local assembly of believers there should be some form of invitation to those suffering from inner trauma, who will then be directed to suitable counselling where they can be transparent and honest and receive informed and compassionate assistance. However, great care must be taken to present the invitation as easily entreated in such a way that it does not drive sufferers into deeper silence. There is a fine line between offering an attractive avenue to pursue help and creating a fear of becoming a public spectacle. How approachable and available are those who could help the silent sufferers?

"Come and let me help you" is the invitation of Christ:

> "*Come unto me, all ye that labour and are heavy laden, and I will give you rest. Take my yoke upon you and learn of me; for I am meek and lowly in heart: and ye shall find rest unto your souls. For my yoke is easy, and my burden is light.*" (Matthew 11:28-30).

Confirm the Pastoral Role

The shepherd's role is to make sure the sheep are doing what the sheep should do. He leads them to a "healthy" pasture of righteousness; they are not driven there.

Jesus' ministry was preaching, teaching, and healing—an interesting integration of activity providing instruction, encouragement, and assistance. Take another look at Matthew 4:24 and notice it states: *"they brought unto him all sick people that were taken with divers diseases and torments,"* What else could the cry of these hurting people be, but *"Help Me!"*

- They were sick and diseased, and they knew it!
- They were hurting and suffering; and they were losing hope, so friends had to bring them!
- They knew they needed help but were not sure where to find it.
- At some point in life, they were moved towards seeking help from the one who could help!

How is it that the church would be able to hear the cries? Would exposure for a couple hours a week at a church service or event be sufficient? Or would engagement and relationship play a greater role? Would the mask of wellness deaden the cries of the hurting or deafen the ears of the believing community? This topic would be worthy of a discussion in any church, especially in the leadership team of the church.

Greg Nelson and Phill McHugh made some significant observations and put them to words in the song they composed, "People Need the Lord."[17] The song has provoked many Christians to serve with compassion in bringing sufferers to Jesus.

Every day they pass me by.
I can see it in their eyes.
Empty people filled with care,
Headed who knows where.
On they go through private pain,
Living fear to fear,
Laughter hides their silent cries,
Only Jesus hears.
People need the Lord, people need the Lord,
At the end of broken dreams, He's the open door.
People need the Lord, people need the Lord,
When will we realize people need the Lord?
We are called to take His light,
To a world where wrong seems right,
What could be too great a cost,
For sharing life with one who's lost?
Through His love our hearts can feel,
All the grief they bear,
They must hear the words of life,
Only we can share.
People need the Lord, people need the Lord.
At the end of broken dreams, He's the open door.
People need the Lord, people need the Lord.
When will we realize that we must give our lives?
For people need the Lord, people need the Lord.

Every line communicates need and opportunity and introduces a real pathway that takes sinners and their helpers from despair to hope!

It hardly needs to be said that the first step in healing is personal reconciliation with God through confession of sin and receiving forgiveness. This eventually leads to personal testimony about the Grace of God, as response to God's Grace becomes evident in worship, in work and in witness. The impact is greatest on others who may need comfort and healing for the ailments that once beset a disciple now on a new and transformative pathway. 2 Corinthians 1:1-7 powerfully outlines this process. In this context each church member could be seen as a "therapist" loving others for the benefit of others!

Application of Pastoral Exposition

Shepherds must be careful to preach clear messages about personal holiness, not presenting it as an impossible mountain to climb, or alternatively, as requiring little attention. The subject is particularly delicate for those harboring traumatic inner scars who may see themselves as fundamentally unholy because of what they have suffered. A message presenting holiness as an easy choice would be deeply discouraging to them.

Perhaps a more effective way to present the subject of holiness is to encourage wounded souls to co-operate with God in a project that He directs—a heavenly Potter who molds earthly clay with great precision and patience. Paul hinted at it in his exhortation to Timothy: *All scripture is given by inspiration of God, and is profitable for doctrine, for reproof, for correction, for instruction in righteousness, that the man of God may be perfect* [matured], *throughly furnished unto all good works.* (2 Timothy 3:16-17).

Consider the description of the poor souls depicted in Matthew 4:23-24 as needing help, and the response from Jesus:

- people that were taken with ***diverse diseases*** (various kinds of debility)
- *and **torments**,* (from the word "basanos," that implies sinking to the bottom, or torture)
- *and those which were **possessed with devils**,* (to be vexed with or possessed by a demon)
- *and those which were **lunatic*** (literally means "moonstruck," that is, mentally ill)
- *and those that **had the palsy*** (a form of paralysis accompanied by tremors)
- *and he healed them.*

The people described here were physically sick, mentally sick, and spiritually sick. They were afflicted in body, soul, and spirit. And Jesus healed them! The word "healed" is from the Greek therapeuō, describing a menial servant waiting on someone as if cherishing them; or to relieve of disease, to cure. Figuratively speaking, it means to adore God![18]

In today's culture we would say, from the description of the people who came to Jesus for healing, that they were all impacted by traumatic events or conditions. The intriguing question challenging Christian ministers is whether healing such sufferers is a sacred or secular issue?

Three Steps to Helping a Traumatized Person:

At the very least, we should consider adopting three positive responses when confronted by someone seeking help: Listen, Validate, Resolve.

Listen – Much of what is called psychotherapy today is about listening, (It is considered in some arenas as "Talk Therapy." In a Christian environment we might go so far as to name it "Soul Therapy"). Listening is allowing someone to express or process their hurt, providing an escape for trapped emotional responses to trauma. It is not uncommon to hear someone say, *"Oh, I am just venting!"* Or perhaps, *"I needed to get that off my chest."* Such comments tell us that an emotional response is being both exercised and excised!

Let the person speak all that is on their heart before answering them. Responding too early may shut the conversation down, and hijack the opportunity for healing. See King Solomon's advice: *He that answereth a matter before he heareth it, it is folly and shame unto him.* (Proverbs 18:13).

Being an attentive listener is a great way to demonstrate interest and respect. What's more, we learn more by listening than by talking. Learning about another person is a very important part of developing a relationship. The most difficult part about attentive listening is minimizing distractions. We achieve this by focusing our attention through listening not only by ear, but also by eye and heart! Listening with the heart reflects our desire to know someone beyond a superficial level, being empathetic, understanding their perspective. Listening with the eye requires us to look in the eye of the one speaking, thereby demonstrating interest for what is being said and valuing the one saying it. We must also avoid distractions from telephones and the like.

Here is some more wisdom from Solomon on this issue:

- *A wise man will hear and will increase learning; and a man of understanding shall attain unto wise counsels: To understand a proverb, and the interpretation; the words of the wise, and their dark sayings.* (Proverbs 1:5-6).
- *The heart of the prudent getteth knowledge; and the ear of the wise seeketh knowledge.* (Proverbs 18:15).
- *My son, attend to my words; incline thine ear unto my sayings. Let them not depart from thine eyes; keep them in the midst of thine heart. For they are life unto those that find them, and health to all their flesh.* (Proverbs 4:20-22).

The New Testament Pastor James had this to say about listening: *Wherefore, my beloved brethren, let every man be swift to hear, slow to speak, slow to wrath: for the wrath of man worketh not the righteousness of God.* (James 1:19).

Practical application of this verse greatly enhances the quality of response!

Validate – This is acknowledgement that provides hope. Validation implies "I hear you and I understand you." It moves someone from a sense of aloneness to acceptance of help. Validation changes the focus. Instead of magnifying the problem, it opens a pathway to a solution. Such healthy reorientation may also eliminate the sense of stigma attached to a particular condition.

Resolve – Once the issue is heard and validated, the conflict that caused the trauma is on the table for resolution. Whether the need is for acceptance or confrontation with an offender, or restitution, the steps toward resolution can be articulated and encouraged because hope is restored and movement in a positive direction can happen!

A final point to make is that addressing problems works better if we ask questions rather than assigning blame, either directly or by inference. Someone has rightly observed that a question stirs the conscience while an accusation hardens the will.

CHAPTER 8

Spiritual Warfare

For we wrestle not against flesh and blood, but against principalities, against powers, against the rulers of the darkness of this world, against spiritual wickedness in high places (Ephesians 6:12).

THE APOSTLE PAUL RECOGNIZED DEMONIC OR devilish activity that wars against us, particularly against our minds. The battle in our mind is a spiritual battle for our soul. Our life and our eternal destiny are the ultimate prize for which the enemies of God contend. Their first intention is to keep us from salvation; after salvation, when we are alive in Christ, they want to render us ineffective in serving our Lord. The battlefield is wide and well-populated.

We must remember that Paul is writing to believers in this current age, the Church Age, or the times of the Gentiles.

We must not relegate spiritual warfare to antiquity. This is a present and relative issue in our day!

The "World"

Paul warned the believers at Colossae: *"Beware lest any man spoil you through philosophy and vain deceit, after the tradition of men, after the rudiments* [foundational principles] *of the world, and not after Christ. For in him dwelleth all the fulness of the Godhead bodily.* (Colossians 2:8-9).

The first appeal to humanity was the devil planting the thought that we could be like God, knowing good and evil, if we followed our own will. So appealing was the thought of having God-like power independent from submission to God that Adam and Eve took the bait! History records that since then the quest for independence has been continuous and brutal, wrought with corruption and heartless; damaging to humanity in every way.

The Apostle Paul's ministry was motivated by a desire to promote the authority and leadership of the Lord Jesus Christ to guide and direct us through life's journey, understanding that the god of this world, the devil, would always contest that leadership! The principle of overcoming spiritual forces arrayed against us was first established in the ministry of Jesus:

> *And the seventy returned again with joy, saying, Lord,* ***even the devils are subject unto us through thy name.*** *And he said unto them, I beheld Satan as lightning fall from heaven.*

*Behold, I give unto you power to tread on serpents and scorpions, and over all the power of the enemy: and nothing shall by any means hurt you. Notwithstanding in this rejoice not **that the spirits are subject unto you:** but rather rejoice, because your names are written in heaven.* (Luke 10:17-20. Emphasis added).

Whether your opinions are formed from ancient history or the evening newscasts, it is evident that the principles of the unregenerate world we live in are anti-God. And therefore we must "beware!"

The "Flesh"

The "works of the flesh"—that is, our fallen human nature—grow out of our selfish desires and appetites. When, as a child of God, we choose to reject the will of God and walk according to our own will, the Holy Spirit of God within us is grieved or quenched. Our actions (works) then produce something other than that which God intends. The complete picture is laid out in Galatians 5:16-26, echoing a principle outlined by Jesus in confrontation with religious hypocrites:

Then came together unto him the Pharisees, and certain of the scribes, which came from Jerusalem. And when they saw some of his disciples eat bread with defiled, that is to say, with unwashen, hands, they found fault. For the Pharisees, and all the Jews, except they wash their hands oft, eat not, holding the tradition of the elders. And when they come from the market, except they wash, they eat not. And many other things there be, which they have received to hold, as the washing of cups, and pots, brazen vessels, and of tables. Then the Pharisees and scribes asked him, Why walk not thy disciples according to the tradition of the elders, but eat bread with unwashen hands? He answered and said unto them, Well hath Esaias prophesied of you hypocrites, as it is written, This people honoureth me with their lips, but their heart is far from me. Howbeit in vain do they worship me, teaching for doctrines the commandments of men [...] Making the word of God of none effect through your tradition...(Mark 7:1-7,13)

Here are some basic truths on the subject, from the Word of God:

- Genesis 8:21 - *.....the imagination of man's heart is evil from his youth.*
- Jeremiah 17:9 - *The heart is deceitful above all things, and desperately wicked: who can know it?*
- I Chronicles 28:17 - *I know also, my God, that thou triest the heart, and hast pleasure in uprightness.*
- Proverbs 23:7 - *For as he thinketh in his heart, so is he.*
- Mark 7: 21-23 – *From within, out of the heart of men, proceed evil thoughts, adulteries, fornications, murders, thefts, covetousness, wickedness, deceit, lasciviousness, an evil eye, blasphemy, pride, foolishness: All these evil things come from within, and defile the man.*

The "Devil"

The third actor in the evil triangle of opposition to God is the Devil. The world, the flesh, and the Devil make a formidable foe! Without inner transformation and ongoing assistance from the Holy Spirit of God, and aided by an invisible army of God's angels, we would not prevail in the battle.

We understand from the story of the Maniac of Gadara (Chapter 3), that demons can possess unbelievers. They can only oppress a born-again believer in Jesus Christ, but that oppression can be relentless in thwarting a healthy relationship with God—especially against those who are weak or damaged in their faith.

The devil's primary tactics include deception, disappointment, discouragement, doubt, and division. The scriptural admonition to oppose the devil is simple:

> *Submit yourselves therefore to God. Resist the devil, and he will flee from you. Draw nigh to God, and he will draw nigh to you. Cleanse your hands, ye sinners; and purify your hearts, ye double minded.* (James 4:7–8).

Submit, resist, draw nigh, cleanse, purify. This is how we effectively resist the devil and win the battle. Notice they are acts of our will and require intention.

The Whole Armor of God

We fight this battle of the mind by employing the tools and tactics presented in the Word of God. Ephesians 6:10-18 lays out the complete strategy, beginning with the admonition to *put on the whole armor of God, that you may be able to stand against the wiles of the devil* (verse 11).

The Expository Files, an online journal dedicated to the faithful exposition of Scripture, edited by Warren E. Berkley & Jon W. Quinn, offers an interesting explanation of the word "wiles" as it applies to the devil's attacks on God's people. A summary of an article written by Berkley is presented here: for the full article, see the link in References ([19]).

> The ways in which the devil "works his craft against us" are enumerated. Our adversary is "the master of wiles" who seeks constantly to "trap us, discourage us and snare us. He will do anything he can do with cunning satanic variety to weaken us and destroy us. He goes to work daily to produce discouragement, confusion, indifference and imbalance.

The article lists four things to watch for in our ongoing spiritual war with the devil.

First, the devil exaggerates the pleasures of sin while minimizing the true nature and outcome of sin.

He asks us to invest in something with promise of immediate return – but without telling us about the risk, the outcome, or the ugly side! If you stop and think, if you inquire; if you look deeply and consider consequences – you frustrate the wiles of the devil. The devil wants us to act on the immediate impulse of the tempted pleasure. The bait looks good, but when you take that bite, you have taken in the ugly poison of sin.

Secondly, the devil sees an opening into our lives through emotions or mood (Ephesians 4:26).

Devils never cease to watch us. When we fall into certain moods or we are overcome by various kinds of emotions, the enemy steps in to defeat us; to lead us into sin.

"When I'm angry and I take that anger with me into the next day, and carry it along with me for weeks and months and years, I might as well wear a bull's eye target. The devil will find me and seek an entrance into my heart for his evil purpose and to my downfall. Use the Word of God and prayer to make a careful inventory of your moods; your emotions; the grudges you carry. Expel the hurt feelings you can't seem to overcome; the habitual, destructive thoughts you entertain, or the devil may use those things to slowly erode your character and your will; to lead you into sin while gradually turning you away from God."

Thirdly, the devil will use people to lead us astray. Jesus said, *Beware of false prophets, who come to you in sheep's clothing, but inwardly they are ravenous wolves.* (Matthew 7:15).

1 Timothy 6:1-5 warns of men who preach and teach and do not maintain loyalty to *"the doctrine which is according to godliness."* When we accept, endorse, and consort with false teachers, that indifference plays right into the hands of error and the devil's purpose. Paul warned Timothy: *From such withdraw yourself.*

And finally, the devil is the master marketing agent

(Hebrews 3:12,13). He knows how to package sin so that it doesn't look like anything bad. This is part of his deceptive essence, to present sin to us in a neat and pretty package so that our first reaction is to look; to admire; to want; to take. How can we stand against such a wily enemy? Scripture provides the answer:

> *Finally, my brethren, be strong in the Lord and in the power of His might. Put on the whole armor of God, that you may be able to stand against the wiles of the devil. For we wrestle not against flesh and blood, but against principalities, against powers, against the rulers of the darkness of this world* [this age], *against spiritual wickedness in high* [heavenly] *places. Therefore take up the whole armor of God, that you may be able to withstand in the evil day, and having done all, to stand. Stand therefore, having girded your waist with truth, having put on the breastplate of righteousness, and having shod your feet with the preparation of the gospel of peace; above all, taking the shield of faith with which you will be able to quench all the fiery darts of the wicked one. And take the helmet of salvation, and the sword of the Spirit, which is the word of God; praying always with all prayer and supplication in the Spirit, being watchful to this end with all perseverance and supplication for all the saints,"* (Ephesians 6:10-18 NKJV).

Paul's letter to the Ephesians admonishes us to change our ways once we are saved. The process of change will be met with much opposition that will come from many directions, but because vital spiritual growth is involved we must adopt the perspective that winning the battle is both the goal and the benefit; both an opportunity and an expectation.

An Opportunity – *Then spake Jesus again unto them, saying, I am the light of the world: he that followeth me shall not walk in darkness, but shall have the light of life.* (John 8:12). A very positive, and appealing opportunity!

An Expectation – *Therefore we are buried with him by baptism into death: that like as Christ was raised up from the dead by the glory of the Father, even so we also should walk in newness of life.* (Romans 6:4.) *For we are his workmanship, created in Christ Jesus unto good works, which God hath before ordained that we should walk in them.* (Ephesians 2:10). In other words, God has a plan!

So, we understand that we have a formidable enemy who seems to be both opportunistic and clever. We also understand that we have a Conquering King in the person of Jesus Christ. As we are "in Christ", we have the power to overcome the enemy. Without Christ we would be completely vulnerable. The King has given us instruction regarding the battle. Our success will be realized as we trust and obey!

CHAPTER 9

Therapeutic Exercises

BEHAVIOR IS DRIVEN BY THOUGHT! BECAUSE EACH of us has a free will, we must take personal responsibility for our thought life (our thinking process) and thought targets. What we feed our mind develops and determines our appetite!

This simple chart highlights a thinking process that is either "life giving" or "life destroying."

Life Giving Thinking	*Life Destroying Thinking*
1. Solution Oriented	1. Problem Oriented
2. Principle driven (facts)	2. Personality driven (feelings)
3. Positive thinking	3. Negative thought
4. Success oriented (I can do all things)	4. Failure oriented (I can't)
5. Think the best (love thinks no evil)	5. Think the worst about someone
6. Discernment	6. Judgment and condemnation
7. Eternal	7. Temporal

Disciplined thinking responds to negative inputs with Biblical Truth, whether from thoughts or circumstances. This follows the example Jesus set when he was tempted in the wilderness. (See Matthew chapter 4, especially verses 4, 7, and 10: *It is written!*)

Consider the Apostle Paul's exhortation to follow this same "therapeutic" practice:

> *For though we walk in the flesh, we do not war after the flesh: (For the weapons of our warfare are not carnal, but mighty through God to the pulling down of strong holds;)* **Casting down imaginations, and every high thing that exalteth itself against the knowledge of God, and bringing into captivity every thought to the obedience of Christ;** *And having in a readiness to revenge all disobedience, when your obedience is fulfilled.* (2 Corinthians 10:3-6. Emphasis added).

God has provided us with appropriate tools! We just need to use them in our efforts to be intentional and disciplined in our way of thinking and in our reactions to the circumstances of life.

Understanding Neural Pathways

When we speak of reactions to circumstances and disciplined thinking it would greatly assist us to understand what this implies, particularly for individuals suffering from PTSD. To this end, here follows a brief introduction to the subject of neural pathways.

A neural pathway may be etched in the brain by repeated trauma. It is a series of connected neurons that send signals from one part of the brain to another. Neurons come in three main types: motor neurons that control muscles; sensory neurons that are stimulated by our senses; and inter-neurons that connect neurons together. These connected neurons process the information we receive. It is these that enable us to interact, and to experience emotions and sensations. They create our memories and enable us to learn from a process that is constantly repeated.

An example of an early neural pathway being formed is seen in a baby's smile. When he or she is rewarded by a smile in return, and possibly a cuddle, the baby learns that smiling is a good thing. Or the same baby may learn that if something sharp is touched, it causes pain. Both encounters are valuable learning experiences and demonstrate the essential nature of neural pathways. However, not all experiences are beneficial. Some may develop pathways that support negative habits.

How Neural Pathways Develop

Like following a physical pathway on the ground, repetition becomes a habit supported by the well-worn path that could be followed with eyes closed. In the same way, always reaching for a bar of chocolate when we feel low, or a drink of alcohol to lessen feelings of anxiety, creates a pathway in the brain that we eventually follow without thinking.

The good news is that the brain can be adjusted to follow different routes or accept different behaviors. This flexibility is called neuroplasticity, and it is this that enables us to change habits that become ingrained. Like the Highways Agency, the brain can create new routes and shut off old ones, with some help and training. [20]

Anxiety

"Phobia" is a fear of something. It is an anxiety characterized as excessive and irrational fear of a specific object, an event, a condition, or a circumstance. This fear can be so intense that it interferes with daily life by causing avoidance behaviors and considerable distress from the thought of returning to a specific circumstance and reliving the experience of physical pain or emotional trauma. It is irrational anticipation that triggers personal anguish by projecting the past into the future and embracing an imaginary outcome; dark, threatening, and hurtful. Uncertainty surrounding the nature of that possibility fuels yet further anxiety.

Such fear is the product of both the former circumstance and the inability at that time to adequately process the fight or flight response. The sufferer was stunned by the event then and is afraid now that there won't be an adequate response or a safe outcome when the next real or imaginary trauma occurs.

Scripture, as usual, has the answers! Paul's instruction to the Philippian believers regarding living an excellent life included an admonition to trust the Lord instead of letting worry sidetrack us. (See Philippians 4:6-9). His action plan to address anxiety was to talk with God about the issues, whatever they are. Instead of being dominated by anxiety, bring the problem to God. Tell Him what you fear and how you feel about it. Ask Him for comfort and resolution, entering the conversation with a spirit of gratitude, knowing that God loves you, cares for you, and can meet your need of the moment. Reject any thought that God will not accept you because the nature and extent of your trauma and your reaction to it may be so personally intimidating—the reality is that God delights in helping those bold enough and desperate enough to seek Him for help! Read Psalm 51 to see how it is done; and rejoice in the fact that as the victim of abuse or emotional torment you stand on firmer ground than David did when he begged for mercy and favor from God, and received it.

After enjoying such a close conversation with God, discipline your thinking accordingly. Verse 9 of Philippians 6 exhorts us to focus on the victorious outcome: "*Those things, which ye have both **learned**, and **received**, and **heard**, and **seen in me*** [learned experience], ***do*** [active experience]: *and the God of peace shall be with you* [inevitable outcome]." Notice the exhortation to move from instruction and knowledge to experience. Rather than merely anticipating a positive outcome, we must trust God, and obey God, and act! The effective result is experiencing the peace of God.

Jesus promised as much:

"Come unto me, all ye that labour and are heavy laden, and I will give you rest. [The Rest of Salvation]. *Take my yoke*

upon you and learn of me; for I am meek and lowly in heart: and ye shall find rest to your souls. [The Rest of Obedience and Service that follows Salvation]. *For my yoke is easy, and my burden is light."* (Matthew 11:28-30).

Recognize that every step of your personal journey after salvation—your highs and lows, your traumas and triumphs, are part of a refining process of spiritual growth intended to conform you to the image of Christ! God has an expected end for your momentary trial that will bring Him glory and fill you with His joy.

Consider this remarkable exhortation:

The Spirit itself beareth witness with our spirit, that we are the children of God; and if children, then heirs; heirs of God and joint-heirs with Christ; if so be that we suffer with Him, that we may be also glorified together [...]*And we know that all things work together for good to them that love God, to them who are the called according to His purpose. For whom He did foreknow, He also did predestinate to be conformed to the image of His Son, that He might be the firstborn among many brethren.* (Romans 8:16-17; 28-29).

As you meditate on the glory and power of these words, cast off the depression that flows from allowing the past to rule your present thoughts. Focus on what you can control—submission to God and His Sovereign Power—and let Him control the rest!

Understanding the Grief Cycle

Persistent, traumatic experiences can cause us to cycle through stages of grief: denial, anger, bargaining, depression, acceptance. These stages may occur in quick succession, or they may be drawn out. Individual responses are unique to personal traits and the specific traumatic injury. Each stage is an attempt to process the experience and protect the sufferer while adapting to a new reality. A reasonable understanding of this process is beneficial for a minister in the process of comforting the suffering.

Denial

When the "fight or flight" emotional response to a traumatic event kicks in, denial quickly follows. It manifests in many ways, including avoidance that feels like shock or procrastination that feels like numbness. *"This can't be happening to me."* Often those in the denial stage are forgetful and feel confused or distracted. They feel like they are shutting down. When asked, they may say, *"I'm fine"* when they clearly are not. It seems as though, while in their confusion, they see no honest response. For the minister, it is helpful to discern between verbal communication and non-verbal communication coming from the sufferer. Observation is important for the one offering aid and comfort. Actions may speak louder than words!

Anger

As the reality of a negative experience sets in, anger rises, along with a sense of pessimism or frustration. An individual may grow impatient and display a "short fuse" reaction to an apparent lack of progress in healing. Offers of help may be met with cynicism or sarcasm and resentment. Irritability and passive-aggressive behavior may also be evident. Outbursts of such negative emotions are upsetting and discouraging for both affected individuals and those trying to help them. Patience will be a friend of the minister in these situations. Understand that this behavior is part of a larger cycle.

Bargaining

The next phase is a sense that progress is being made towards normalization of reasonable thinking. Negotiation with inner thoughts and reactions in pursuit of normalization is called "bargaining" in the Grief Cycle, drawing from the past while looking to the future. Counter-productive emotions at this stage include self-blame, sorrow, and then fear and anxiety from assuming the worst for the future. A growing sense of failure, regret and insecurity may be overwhelming, giving rise to comments like, "I should have…" or "If only…" For the one ministering to the sufferer, presence, compassion, and demonstrations of love may be more powerful than any words you can speak.

Depression

Depression is the inevitable result of harsh inner criticism. An overwhelming sense of sadness and despair may lead to sleep disorders or eating disorders, and appetite changes. This can manifest physically in reduced energy. Hopelessness leads to withdrawal from social interests and even isolation. Sufferers appear to have no motivation and resist the motivation others may offer.

In depression, the disappointment and pain may cause crying. When suffering becomes unbearable alcohol or drugs may be sought as an immediate form of relief. It is not healthy for people to stay in this stage of the grief cycle for very long. Expressions of encouragement and support towards a better tomorrow may bring some comfort through this phase. Sincerity will add to their effectiveness.

Acceptance

There comes a point when the sufferer at last embraces the realities of traumatic events and responses and understands their experience. In this crucial stage of grief resolution, hope is formed that the impacts of past events have lost their power. A "fight or flight response" is no longer necessary. They can now take a deep breath and rejoice in their survival! This brings a sense of validation and courage to face the future. A positive view of life is broadened by learning new coping mechanisms. They are now equipped to comfort others who may tread the same pathway of silent suffering. They have learned from their past and can now look toward the future while living today.

Accepting Comfort and Consolation

When we hurt or suffer and allow others to comfort and console us we should be open to the truth that God is preparing us to comfort someone else. We may look beyond our own little picture to God's bigger picture. There is a purpose to our suffering that may well have nothing to do with "punishment" and everything to do with enlightening others.

Consider these opening remarks from the Apostle Paul's second letter to the church in Corinth:

> *Blessed be God, even the Father of our Lord Jesus Christ, the Father of mercies, and the God of all comfort; Who comforteth us in all our tribulation, that we may be able to comfort them which are in any trouble,* **by the comfort wherewith we ourselves are comforted of God.** *For as the sufferings of Christ abound in us, so* **our consolation also aboundeth by Christ.** *And whether we be afflicted, it is for your consolation and salvation, which is effectual in the enduring of the same sufferings which we also suffer: or whether we be comforted, it is for your consolation and salvation. And our hope of you is stedfast, knowing that as ye are partakers of the sufferings, so shall ye be also of the consolation.* (2 Corinthians 1:3-7. Emphasis added).

As we experience the consoling love of Jesus Christ in our suffering, it is preparing us to be effectual [actively powerful] in ministry to others who are suffering. It is truths like this that help us realize that God's plan is so much bigger than our little minds can comprehend. He is the Almighty, the all Powerful, and the all-Knowing God.

Commonly Recognized Treatments and Remedies

From my research I have identified commonly recognized treatments for mental illness that typically include a combination of therapy, medication, lifestyle changes, and systemic planning. A specific treatment plan will depend on the type and severity of the mental illness. While not an exhaustive list, I want to acknowledge some mainstream approaches to dealing with mental health issues, as a guide to an individual's further research. Part of the decision-making process should include consultation with a pastor or Christian counsellor whose assistance is gained at the outset of the journey towards inner healing and spiritual growth. The common treatments are:

Psychotherapy – This is often referred to as "Talk Therapy." Some prominent modalities include:

- Cognitive Behavioral Therapy (CBT): A therapy that helps individuals identify and change negative thought patterns.
- Dialectical Behavior Therapy (DBT): A therapy considered effective for borderline personality disorder and emotional regulation.
- Psychodynamic Therapy: A therapy that explores past experiences and unconscious processes.
- Interpersonal Therapy (IPT): A therapy with a focus on improving relationships and communication.

Medication

- Antidepressants: Medications used for depression and anxiety disorders (e.g., SSRIs like fluoxetine, SNRIs like venlafaxine). [21] Selective serotonin reuptake inhibitors, also called SSRIs, are the type of antidepressant prescribed most often. They can ease symptoms of moderate to severe depression. They are considered relatively safe, and they typically cause fewer side effects than other antidepressants.

- How SSRIs work - Serotonin is one of many chemical messengers in the brain called neurotransmitters. Neurotransmitters carry signals between nerve cells in the brain, called neurons. After carrying a signal between brain cells, serotonin usually is taken back into those cells; a process called reuptake. SSRIs block this process. Blocking reuptake makes more serotonin available to help pass messages between brain cells. SSRIs are called selective because they mainly affect serotonin, not other neurotransmitters. SSRIs may be used to treat conditions other than depression, such as anxiety disorders.

- Antipsychotics: Medications that are often prescribed to treat schizophrenia and bipolar disorder (e.g., risperidone, olanzapine).

- Mood Stabilizers: Medications that help manage mood swings in bipolar disorder (e.g., lithium, valproate).

- Anxiolytics (Anti-Anxiety Medications): Medications used

to help with anxiety disorders (e.g., benzodiazepines, often used short-term).

Lifestyle and Self-Care

- Exercise: Regular physical activity improves mood and reduces stress.
- Healthy Diet: Nutrient-rich foods support brain function.
- Sleep Hygiene: Maintaining a regular sleep schedule is crucial for mental well-being.

Mindfulness & Meditation:

- Techniques such as deep breathing and meditation help with stress management.

Support Systems

- Family and Friends: Emotional support from loved ones can aid in recovery.
- Support Groups: Peer-led groups (e.g., Alcoholics Anonymous, NAMI [National Alliance on Mental Illness] support groups) provide shared experiences and encouragement.

Community Services: Mental health organizations offer counseling, crisis intervention, and rehabilitation programs.

Hospitalization or Intensive Treatment (For Severe Cases)

- Inpatient Care: Short-term hospitalization for crisis situations.
- Day Programs (Partial Hospitalization): Intensive therapy without full hospitalization. These may be referred to as "outpatient programs."

Electroconvulsive Therapy (ECT): Used in severe cases of depression when other treatments fail.

Non-medicinal Therapies

Non-medicinal therapies are exercises that require disciplined application and repetition. Here are two examples:

- **Breathing** – One of the first exercises I was taught while in therapy for my PTSD was breathing. I learned to respond to an oncoming sense of anxiety by taking slow, deep breaths that slowed the world around me and brought a sense of calmness.
- **Grounding** – Consider this example from the University of Arizona: "Grounding yourself in a safe space can help you reconnect with the present moment. Look for a spot that feels steadying or comforting to you. It might be:
  - Sitting on the floor and feeling the ground beneath you.
  - Standing in sunlight and letting the warmth remind you of the here and now.

- Stepping outside to feel the air on your skin and hear the sounds around you."[22]

Doctors and therapists are usually trained in a myriad of non-medicinal exercises. Again, those in treatment will discover that the effectiveness of the exercises is determined by how intentionally and disciplined they follow the prescribed courses of treatment.

Mentioning these common therapies is not intended to be an endorsement of them by the author. While they may be an appropriate path forward for some, they may also become a substitute for the treatment provided by God and His Word.

A FINAL THOUGHT

THERE IS A SIGNIFICANT DIFFERENCE BETWEEN LIFE in a fantasy world and living in the real world. Textbook theory does not hit home until we experience real life. James, in chapter 2 of his epistle, touched this reality when he said, *"faith without works is dead."* It was dead because it was alone! Faith, untested by reality, seems empty! **Theory needs experience to validate it.** Knowing and doing are two different things. We might say **the bridge from theory to reality is experience;** trusting and obeying!

If you are stuck in the past, ruminating on theoretical and fearful possibilities, and you are looking across the deep canyon of despair that separates you from the real help and hope that abides on the other side, ask the Lord to give you courage and strength to get on the bridge of experience and make your way into a victorious reality.

Trust and Obey! Trust God and obey His Word! I wonder if the believing community thinks too lightly of this "treatment." When the Apostle Paul says, *"So then faith cometh by hearing, and   hearing by the word of God,"* (Romans 10:17), he is implying that one who knows their experience, and connects their experience to what God has said in His Word, develops faith—that is, confidence in God, leading to further trust! And we further build our faith when we continue to read God's Word, while the indwelling Holy Spirit supports the mind—our heart! Everyday events become enlightening moments to deepen our faith relationship with God as we connect experience and Truth.

A key element in this process is recognizing the works of God. The Apostle Paul wrote to the Roman believers: *For whatsoever things were written aforetime* [the Old Testament for the Roman audience, the whole Bible for us today] *were written for our learning, that we* **through patience and comfort of the scriptures** *might have* **hope.** (Romans 15:4. Emphasis added).

We can see in the pages of Scripture how God worked in the lives of others back then, and it teaches us how God works today, because God doesn't change. This truth gives us hope!

Knowing how God works will help us to realize we are "God's workmanship" (Ephesians 2:10). Knowing He is at work, and that He is always working for His glory and our benefit (Romans 8:28), builds our trust in Him. Accompanying that trust is "the peace of God."

This truth is captured so well in a poem written by Mary Stevenson[23] titled: "Footprints In The Sand."

One night I dreamed I was walking along the beach
with the Lord.
Many scenes from my life flashed across the sky.
In each scene I noticed footprints in the sand.
Sometimes there were two sets of footprints,
other times there were one set of footprints.

This bothered me because I noticed
that during the low periods of my life,
when I was suffering from
anguish, sorrow or defeat,
I could see only one set of footprints.

So I said to the Lord,
"You promised me Lord,
that if I followed you,
you would walk with me always.
But I have noticed that during
the most trying periods of my life
there have only been one
set of footprints in the sand.
Why, when I needed you most,
you have not been there for me?"

The Lord replied,
"The times when you have
seen only one set of footprints,
is when I carried you."

To experience this peace, take God at His Word, and trust him to the point of obedience. Put Him to the test in your life. He wants you to do that because He loves you and cares for you and desires that you grow spiritually strong in your relationship with Him.

C.S. Lewis said that healing is a journey. It is in times of testing and distress that we draw close to God—we come to know Him better, and know His Word better, and know ourselves better. The first five verses of Psalm 30 provide a powerful framework for meditation on the journey towards healing, and bring a fitting conclusion to the brief insight this book offers into the healing of broken souls.

¹I will extol thee, O Lord; for thou hast lifted me up, and hast not made my foes to rejoice over me. ²O Lord my God, I cried unto thee, and thou hast healed me. ³O Lord, thou hast brought up my soul from the grave: thou hast kept me alive, that I should not go down to the pit.

⁴Sing unto the Lord, O ye saints of his, and give thanks at the remembrance of his holiness. ⁵For his anger endureth but a moment; in his favour is life: weeping may endure for a night, but joy cometh in the morning.

ABOUT THE AUTHOR

DR. MIKE DUFFY and his wife of fifty-seven years have three children together, twelve grandchildren, and five great-grandchildren. Mike's life experience is characterized by service, integrity, leadership, and accomplishment. He grew up in a home that was shattered by alcoholism when he was in elementary school. Overcoming this tragedy and trauma early in life, he has experienced productivity and success on many levels.

Mike is a combat veteran who served a tour in Vietnam with an infantry battalion of the United States Army's Eighty-Second Airborne Division. He learned early the value and reward of working hard and excelled in a corporate career for fourteen years in administrative management and sales, receiving international awards at each level for outstanding achievement and accomplishment.

Dr. Duffy received Jesus Christ as his personal Savior at age thirty-one and committed his life to Christian ministry at age thirty-five, ministering God's Word in nearly one thousand ministries nationally and internationally.

The following statement from Mike reveals his heart: "There is trauma and tragedy everywhere. I believe that everyone will face some adversity in life. How one responds to that adversity will shape their future. People can be paralyzed, damaged, or destroyed when adversity comes, or they can use adversity as motivation for positive change. We cannot change the past, but we do not have to live there either. We must learn from the past, look toward the future, but live today. Although no one can go back and change their beginning, they can begin today to change their ending. This is what hope looks like. I love serving God and others and have found that this approach in life is the pathway to happiness.

Mike has authored several books and hundreds of articles published in his *My Library of Life* which can be found on his website: www.drmikeduffy.com.

ENDNOTES

1   Rosaria C. Butterfield – *The Secret Thoughts of an Unlikely Convert* - Crown & Covenant Publications, Pittsburgh, PA 15208, 2012–Chapter 2

2   Rosaria C. Butterfield – *The Secret Thoughts of an Unlikely Convert* - Crown & Covenant Publications, Pittsburgh, PA 15208, 2012 –Chapter 1

3   Strong's Greek Lexicon, "G2560," Blue Letter Bible, accessed August 9, 2025, https://www.blueletterbible.org/lexicon/g2560/kjv/tr/0-1/.

4   Strong's Greek Lexicon, "G4982," Blue Letter Bible, accessed August 9, 2025, https://www.blueletterbible.org/lexicon/g4982/nkjv/tr/0-1/

5   Cambridge Dictionary, definition of "mental," accessed August 9, 2025 https://dictionary.cambridge.org/us/dictionary/english/mental

6   Classic Sermons On A Timeless Topic: Spiritual Depression – Amazon Marketing Commentary about D. Martyn Lloyd-Jones' book *Spiritual Depression: Its Causes and Cures* - 1998, Zondervan. Kindle Edition, accessed August 9, 2025, https://www.amazon.com/Spiritual-Depres%20-%20sion-Its-Causes-Cure/dp/0802813879

7   HarperCollins, Lloyd-Jones, David Martyn. *Spiritual Depression: Its Causes and Cures* - 1998, Zondervan. Kindle Edition.

8   Strong's Greek Lexicon, "G227," Blue Letter Bible, accessed August 9, 2025, https://www.blueletterbible. org/lexicon/g227/kjv/tr/0-1/

9   Strong's Greek Lexicon, "G4586," Blue Letter Bible, accessed August 9, 2025, https://www.blueletterbible. org/lexicon/g4586/kjv/tr/0-1/

10   Strong's Greek Lexicon, "G1342," Blue Letter Bible, accessed August 9, 2025, https://www.blueletterbible. org/lexicon/g1342/kjv/tr/0-1/

11   Strong's Greek Lexicon, "G53," Blue Letter Bible, accessed August 9, 2025, https://www.blueletterbible. org/lexicon/g53/kjv/tr/0-1/

12   Strong's Greek Lexicon, "G4375," Blue Letter Bible, accessed August 9, 2025, https://www.blueletterbible. org/lexicon/g4375/kjv/tr/0-1/

13   Strong's Greek Lexicon, "G2163," Blue Letter Bible, accessed August 9, 2025, https://www.blueletterbible. org/lexicon/g2163/kjv/tr/0-1/

14   Strong's Greek Lexicon, "G3049," Blue Letter Bible, accessed August 9, 2025, https://www.blueletterbible. org/lexicon/g3049/kjv/tr/0-1/

15   Strong's Greek Lexicon, "H2416," Blue Letter Bible, accessed August 9, 2025, https://www.blueletterbible. org/lexicon/h2416/kjv/wlc/0-1/

16   Strong's Greek Lexicon, "G3619," Blue Letter Bible, accessed August 9, 2025, https://www.blueletterbible. org/lexicon/g3619/kjv/tr/0-1/

17   Greg Nelson and Phil McHugh "*People Need the Lord*" 1983

18   Strong's Greek Lexicon, ' G2323," Blue Letter Bible, accessed August 9, 2025, https://www.blueletterbible.org/lexicon/g2323/kjv/tr/0-1/

19   The Interactive Bible, accessed August 9, 2025, https://www.bible.ca/ef/expository-ephesians-6-11.htm

20   Great Minds Clinic Blog, *What Are Neural Pathways*, accessed August 9, 2025, https://www.greatmindsclinic.co.uk/blog/what-are-neural-pathways/

21   Mayo Clinic, *Selective Serotonin Reuptake Inhibitors (SSRIs)*, accessed August 9, 2025, https://www.mayoclinic.org/diseases-conditions/depression/in-depth/ssris/art-20044825

22   University of Arizona, *Grounding Strategies*, accessed August 9, 2025, https://caps.arizona.edu/grounding#thoughts

23   Mary Stevenson, Footprints In The Sand, Accessed August 9, 2025, https://thebottomofabottle.wordpress.com/2013/03/23/footprints-in-the-sand-by-mary-stevenson/